LEARNING
TO
WORSHIP

LEARNING
TO
WORSHIP

Edna M. Baxter

THE JUDSON PRESS
Valley Forge

LEARNING TO WORSHIP

I will pray with the Spirit and I will pray with my mind also; I will sing with the Spirit and I will sing with my mind also.

—1 Corinthians 14:15

DEDICATED
TO MY FORMER COLLEAGUES AND STUDENTS
AT THE HARTFORD SCHOOL OF RELIGIOUS EDUCATION

Foreword

DURING MANY YEARS OF WORKING with pastors, religious educators, missionaries, and laymen, the author discovered endless need for genuine guidance in worship. Resources for such work are scattered or nonexistent.

Seminaries generally focus on the minister in the pulpit and the services which he leads. After studying in several important seminaries, the author sensed the neglect and began to work on worship education for laymen as well as professional leaders. Guidance of theological students in their work with laymen who lead the worship among all age groups in the churches demands careful planning and thought. Much material had to be created.

Whatever children learn about worship and prayer comes largely (if at all) from parents or church teachers. Too often such worship is highly abstract and symbolic. Leaders of children need a great deal of guidance and preparation in order to make their work with young folks helpful.

It has been found that worship and prayer in our churches is often confusing and even meaningless. This difficulty is allied to a great deal of theological confusion. If people are to grow to accept God's will and purpose for all realms of their lives, they will require much more guidance and preparation in our Protestant churches.

In order to help leaders of laymen, the author began preparing and gathering meaningful resources for students in the theological seminary and for schools for laymen. Some of these are now placed in *Learning to Worship*.

It is the author's belief that laymen from churches "on mission" in a material and secular world must have help in keeping their lives centered in God's love and purpose whereever they are. There is a special need today for a new vision of worship and its meaning.

It is hoped that parents, church teachers of all ages, adult and professional leaders will find inspiration and guidance in this book.

Sincere thanks are due to many students who attended my classes and worked with me individually in their laboratory work in teaching.

Special thanks are due to the late Phyllis Maramarco, an able religious educator and musician, who helped greatly in the section on music and permitted me to quote two of her original hymns and other material. Thanks are due also to Professor John F. Bullough for advice on music and to Dean Estella Lane for the use of her story.

EDNA M. BAXTER

Contents

PART ONE: MEANING AND PRACTICE OF WORSHIP

1.
Worship and Life

THE ESSENCE OF RELIGION IS WORSHIP, and the heart of worship is prayer, says Herbert H. Farmer.[1] Through such experiences our wills may be brought into likeness to the will of God and "to the purification of our desires, the cleansing of our motives and the strengthening of our relationship with Him."[2]

People need to be united with the creative, sustaining spirit and energy of God. His will needs to be acknowledged in every aspect and realm of life. Paul wrote to the Romans: "Do not be conformed to this world but be transformed by the renewal of your mind, that you may prove what is the will of God, what is good and acceptable and perfect" (Romans 12:2).

Surrender to God provides endless room for our growth. Adoration of and devotion to God involves adoration of God's loving purpose and righteous will. The fruits of this spirit will be "love, joy, peace, patience, kindness, goodness, faith-

[1] See *Revelation and Religion*, by Herbert H. Farmer, professor emeritus of Cambridge University (New York: Harper & Row, 1954).

[2] *Rethinking the Christian Message*, by Norman Pittenger (New York: Seabury Press, Inc., 1956).

fulness, gentleness, self-control," says Paul (Galatians 5:22-23).
Children as well as adults need to learn that God does not
speak "out loud" or through an "angel visitant," or "opening
skies." Genuine fellowship with God requires time and practice. Then can come an awareness of his will and his purpose. To be real, the worshiper must act out in all his relationships this vision of love and justice. God will seem nearest
when living is carried on according to his spirit. Then we
become truly God's temples. The late Dr. David E. Roberts
has wisely said that Protestantism rests on the principle that
it is possible to relate all human accomplishments, continually
and invisibly, to God.

We learn from God by close fellowship and concentration.
True worship is rooted in the acceptance of God as reality;
it requires time, discipline, and effort on the part of the
worshiper. Concepts of God need to be Christian, for we find
our best understanding of God through Jesus. God should
become central in all that we do. As Jesus said, "You shall
worship the Lord your God and him only shall you serve"
(Matthew 4:10).

True worship should enable man to know God in God's
way—not according to tradition, not in terms of orthodoxy,
not in terms of one's own peace of mind. Sentimental songs,
poems, exercises, and hollow forms and ceremonies may be
injurious.

PERSPECTIVE

Worship can remind us of central points of view and promote perspective, making great things look great, and small
things look small.

Worship may involve a repeated and continuous weighing
of issues and results, together with the development of new
activities that arise in changing situations.[3] Involved in these
experiences is the need of the worshiper to broaden and

[3] See Chapter 5.

sharpen his perspective and discrimination in one ethical area after another. His faults and those of groups of people must be reevaluated and tested from God's point of view. Children, young people, and adults all require this constant weighing of issues and this testing of motives and actions in the light of God's spirit. They can then begin to hear the voice of God above the noise of selfish struggle and find an eternal moral order, supported by God. The keynote of worship may be said to be the union of God with man and of man with God.

In the midst of the conflicts of modern life and the ever-widening vistas of science, the worshiper needs to seek the truth and to learn in God's spirit how to use today's new data on God's terms. One step can lead to another in the realms of justice and righteousness—social, economic, interracial, and international. Customs, traditions, and mores thus may need to be opposed, for lofty worship can hardly encourage reconciliation with injustice and the evils of the day, nor can it lead to smugness, submission, or escape. Genuine devotion to God will involve the facing of our faults leading to repentance and the amendment of conduct; unpopular causes may involve suffering love. Jesus truly said, "If you love me, you will keep my commandments" (John 14:15), and again, "By this all men will know that you are my disciples, if you have love for one another" (John 13:35).

Worship, then, is not some ceremony or petition to change God. God's ways are orderly, dependable, and eternal. It is finite man who is to be changed. Man is to become a creator with God; man is to decide to give over his will and spirit to the infinite will and spirit of God; man is to give all of his purposes and motives into the keeping of God. Arthur Holt [4] has well said that "modern worship is not intended

---

[4] *This Nation Under God,* by Arthur E. Holt (Chicago: Willett, Clarke & Co., 1939), p. 183.

as an attempt to influence the purposes of God, but rather as a technique for understanding them." At the outset in all worship, God is completely central and all-pervading.

Lofty, sincere worship will lead to a harmonious relationship with God in varied aspects of life. There will be sincerity without pretense. Form and pretense can be tested by their fruits in family and community living, race relationships, treatment of all kinds of people, and the way one views his own life. God as we know him through Jesus is the God of history, of nations, and of peoples, as well as of individuals. It is his will that is to become actual among men and that is to be accepted in every aspect of life. Since all the resources of the earth are gifts of God, so every type of ownership or possession should be kept under scrutiny, that it may not distort the purposes of God's creation. Man's freedom begins when he recognizes himself as a co-worker with God and when he allows God to become the center and dynamic of his living. All social progress requires sanctions beyond the self-centered and selfish—those which are rooted in God's eternal order. With such insight man can be united with the creative spirit and energy of God. A proper kind of humility can develop as man seeks the truth and gains fresh confidence due to his vision of God. Not man's will but God's will becomes the goal of life.

PURPOSE OF WORSHIP

The gospel challenges us to submit all of our lives to God: our ambitions, our wills, our motives, and our activities (Romans 12:1). We are to submit our ways of living to the source of all meaning and values and to a judge beyond our self-esteem and the pressures of people. God requires more than self-centeredness, pretension, and complacency.

True worship should enable us to become aware of our true selves. In it there is no false humility or self-obsession, no self-abasement, self-accusation, or pride. In genuine wor-

ship we need to grow in our capacity to think with God about our failures, wrong decisions, apathy, indifference to the welfare of others, and all other wrongdoing. Out of this experience will come confession and the sincere seeking of forgiveness.

In worship we should weigh and evaluate the potentialities for good which are present in actual situations, as well as the points where wrong could have been avoided. From such experiences can come resolution to seek and to accept or to be guided by God's spirit. The continuous yielding of our wills and lives to God brings communion and greater harmony with God. Thanksgiving and praise to God and a renewed perspective on daily living are aspects of worship that unite us with God in friendship and communion (Psalm 145:1-3). Worship enables us to be taught by God.

The late William Temple, Archbishop of Canterbury, has well said:

> This world can be saved . . . by one thing only and that is worship. . . . Companionship with Him is worship. . . .
> For to worship is to quicken the conscience by the holiness of God, to feed the mind with the truth of God, to purge the imagination by the beauty of God, to open the heart to the love of God, to devote the will to the purpose of God. . . . Those who pray as Christ taught us to pray . . . do not pray that their own will may be done, but God's. . . . It is the dedication of ourselves . . . to the Father.[5]

WORKING WITH GOD IN ALL SITUATIONS

The recognition of God in the *now* of life needs to receive much more attention by Christians, particularly in the education of children and youth. Many aspects of life are treated today as secular and material without any relation to God as the source of all things or as involving the will of the God of the universe. Children frequently think of God as limited to

[5] *The Hope of a New World,* by William Temple (New York: Macmillan Co., 1941), pp. 26, 28, 30, 35. Used by permission of Mrs. William Temple.

church buildings. In one class of fifth-grade children, most of them said, "God is only found in church." A group of adolescents declared, "This is the first time that we have realized that God has anything to do with life outside the church." As early as the fourth grade, children say, "We do not see how God has anything to do with the science we learn about in our science classes."

Biblical religion reflects a people associating God with many aspects of their lives. Though their science was defective in the light of present knowledge and thinking, they continued to associate God with their total world view. The Psalms are full of this awareness as are the records in the Bible of individual, social, and national affairs of the Hebrew people.

Such recognition and devotion to the God of the universe, as he has been revealed to us, needs to become an important part of Christian education.

GOD AND DISASTER

In dealing with the religious questions of children as well as adults, it is clear that most of these grow out of life's experiences. When something hard or threatening happens, someone will ask, "Why has God done this to me?" Recently, the author heard some bright, sixth-grade children from church families saying that it was God's plan for the people to be killed in a plane that was destroyed by a bomb carried intentionally by one of the passengers, or placed there by some other person. Not one child in this group of children recognized the part man's freedom has in God's plan. Instead, they ascribed all kinds of unpleasant events to God's intention.

GROWTH IN A SENSE OF WORTH AND RESPONSIBILITY

God's love for mankind reveals that people have worth and are precious. So the worshiper should come to feel his own worth and significance. He stands in relation to the God who cares about his choices, his relationships, and the way man works out his vocation. His decisions, his point of view, and his behavior are really significant. Man is not "a worm in the dust"; he has potential to become Godlike.

Such a sense of worth must lead the worshiper out of self-centeredness into devotion and dedication to the truth and to God's purposes in life around him. There is great power in joining other worshipers of the church in this outreach to God. No man can live unto himself alone. Each genuine worshiper becomes the living contact at which the power of God can touch and influence the life around him.

The true and sincere worshiper of God will not escape from the world around him; there is great danger in a wholly other-world view. Redemption involves men's bodies as well as their souls, and genuine worship should make room for the material and social concerns of life. The worshiper will perceive what he ought to do and at the same time should grow in God's spirit to do it.

George Albert Coe, who wrote so effectively on worship, has said that suitable worship can save our goodness from overassertiveness, overstrenuousness, and angularity by making us aware of the quality of God's spirit. Our desires must be turned towards objectives outside of self and in terms of the love of God towards people in every situation in life.

EDUCATION IN WORSHIP

Inasmuch as worship is central for the Christian, the schools of the church need to provide more adequate education and experience for all age-levels, including adults.

The author has been constantly faced by church people of all ages who have not known how to pray. In the Second World War, for instance, it was found that many of the men were unprepared to pray. Some had learned one childish prayer and that seemed to be all that they had.

Prayer should be taught through adult example and witness, and through thinking and experience, to all children and young people. They can learn to pray at table, at the beginning and the end of the day, on entering a church, in crises, in moments of triumph and joy, and in all of life. Such prayer is much more than "saying prayers," though good ones can help people to learn the spirit and language of prayer.

Both formal and informal worship need to be taught in the church school. Participation in leadership should be introduced very gradually only as all of a group will benefit rather than just the leader. Worship is a high art.

Persons of all ages who lead or guide worship services should have much preparation for their participation. The chapters which follow are planned for the guidance of leaders in Protestant churches. Baptism and communion are not included, however, because they should receive considerable historical review and sufficient space for a full description of the various ways in which these events take place.

2.
The God We Worship

WHEN PEOPLE OF ANY AGE are learning to worship God, they
need much help through formal training sessions and informal
interpretation of their own worship experiences, to understand something of the nature of God as revealed in the Bible
and in the universe and how he can help us to pray.[1]

GOD REACHES PEOPLE

Basically, the Christian needs to understand that "It is
he [God] that made us . . ." (Psalm 100:3b). At the same time
people have been given capacity to be reached by God
(Romans 2:14-16). In this respect we are unlike plants, trees,
and animals. God has planned for man to know him. We
read in Romans 1:20: "Ever since the creation of the world
his invisible nature, namely, his eternal power and deity, has
been clearly perceived in the things that have been made."
We see God's work "in the things that have been made."

The Creator is evident in all his creation (Psalm 104) and
in the order which he sustains. Younger people should begin

[1] See *How to Pray*, by Jean-Nicolas Grou, tr. by Joseph Dalby, D.D.
(New York: Harper & Row, 1956).

to learn to recognize that God is creative and at work today as well as in the past. This is God's world. He is continuously active in it. Worship involves such recognition of God at work by giving thanks and praise for that which we do see or experience. We should never allow some mechanical view of nature to crowd out the glory of God as its creator and sustainer. From God's standpoint all is sacred. We should "remember the wonderful works that he has done" (Psalm 105:5a) and continually "tell of all his wonderful works!" (Psalm 105:2b). The Old Testament reminds us that God is the creator of the heavens and the earth. Paul declared "the earth is the Lord's, and everything in it" (1 Corinthians 10:26). In John 1:3 we read, "all things were made through him, and without him was not anything made that was made." Likewise, Job in the Old Testament continuously recognizes this relationship (Job 37:4).

At every moment, man should recognize that he is dependent upon his Creator. God works through all the myriad channels of life and order. Man has been made for God—for God's glory and for fellowship with God. The radiant, joyful life comes when people live for God and his purposes.

GOD'S WILL

God's purpose can be met in all events, yet no evil can be attributed to God's will in any form. God does not will everything that happens, but he wills what *should* happen. His love is always available, and persons can be affected and changed by it if they will accept God's purposes. The Christian needs to reject the constant refrain that "God wills it" in so many situations in life. Through worship and prayer he may become at one with God's love.

GOD SUSTAINS ORDER

The experiences of people, the studies of sciences, and the teachings of biblical writers all acknowledge that there is, on the whole, an orderly system in the universe. God makes himself known as the dependable and reliable creator and sustainer of it. "He makes his sun rise on the evil and on the good" (Matthew 5:45b).

The physical and the spiritual life are subject to this order. Man has to learn to live in it and to use it for God's purposes. He must make decisions about how to carry out the love of God in infinite ways. None of us is *compelled* to be honest, reliable, or helpful, but the rule of God makes his will the only right and acceptable way to live on this planet. "The sum of thy word is truth . . ." (Psalm 119:160).

God is unchanging from age to age. His will, his love never cease. There is no place where he is not at work (Psalm 139:8-10,13). "In him we live and move and have our being" (Acts 17:28a).

NATURE OF GOD

God is one (1 Corinthians 8:4) and is a conscious, willing personality.

> . . . I am God, and there is no other;
> I am God, and there is none like me,
> . . . My counsel shall stand,
> and I will accomplish all my purpose.
>
> — *Isaiah* 46:9-10

Paul says, "No one comprehends the thoughts of God except the Spirit of God" (1 Corinthians 2:11b). God is particularly referred to in the New Testament as Father and as love. His power is the power of love. Man can know God best by living in harmony with his will and spirit.

GOD WORKS IN PEOPLE

"No man has ever seen God" (1 John 4:12a). "God is love, and he who abides in love abides in God, and God abides in him" (1 John 4:16b). God works in and through people when we can see some of his beauty, truth, and goodness.

These qualities show God at work in many of the people that we find in the Bible.

James says we "are made in the likeness of God" (James 3:9b). We resemble God in that we have capacity to live as his children. Like God, man can reason, think, will, and choose. He is aware of good and evil. He lives in a world of meaning. He fulfills his own nature when he participates with God in God's own perfection. Jesus said, "You, therefore, must be perfect, as your heavenly Father is perfect" (Matthew 5:48).

It is important to grow in a vital, living relationship to God, who is the creating source of the universe, of people, and of all good.

THE CHARACTER OF GOD IN JESUS

The church worships God as revealed in Jesus as the Son (Hebrews 1:3). Luther said, "We find the heart and will of the Father in Christ." In Christ we have our most complete understanding of God (Matthew 11:27), for his teachings and life reveal God's love, goodness, and majesty (John 1:14), and his will was freely and wholly yielded to God. Thus in Jesus the will of a man and of God were met in one purpose for all mankind (Luke 4:18-19 and John 14:9).

TESTING OUR OWN LIVES

The life and teachings of Jesus aid us in testing our own lives. We read in the First Letter of John, to "test the spirits to see whether they are of God . . ." (1 John 4:1b). From the words of Jesus we can ascertain some of these tests: "You are my friends if you do what I command you" (John 15:14). "This I command you, to love one another" (John 15:17). "By this all men will know that you are my disciples, if you have love for one another" (John 13:35). "He who says he abides in him ought to walk in the same way in which he walked" (1 John 2:6). "He who says he is in the light and hates his brother is in the darkness still" (1 John 2:9). "Little children, let us not love in word or speech but in deed and in truth" (1 John 3:18).

In communion with God there is a creation of divine love. In this communion there can come testimony of the Holy Spirit: "The Spirit himself bearing witness with our spirit," writes Paul (Romans 8:16). Divine will can thus enter man's life in the affairs of the world. Paul urges the Romans to be "transformed by the renewal of your mind, that you may prove what is the will of God, what is good and acceptable and perfect" (Romans 12:2).

GOD'S LOVE AT WORK

The Christian must be motivated by his love of God and his acceptance of the meaning of God as shown in Jesus as the Christ. Love of God and love of people are a basic part of the Christian life (Mark 12:29-31).

"You are my friends," says Jesus in John 15:14, if you keep God's commandments. A new spirit grows in the mind and thought of people when God's ways take root. Paul says, "We know that in everything God works for good with those who love him, who are called according to his purpose" (Romans 8:28). "Let love be genuine; hate what is evil, hold fast to what is good; love one another with brotherly affection; . . . be aglow with the Spirit . . . be constant in prayer" (Romans 12:9,10,11b,12b). Paul wrote to the Galatians that "the fruit of the Spirit is love, joy, peace, patience, kindness, goodness, faithfulness, gentleness, self-control. . . . If we live by the Spirit let us walk by the Spirit. Let us have no self-conceit, no provoking of one another, no envy of one another" (Galatians 5:22,23,25,26).

When people accept God's love and will, they can face all of life in a special way, and their lives will show godliness in their actions.

In the letter of James, he stresses that we "be doers of the word, and not hearers only, deceiving yourselves. . . . What does it profit, my brethren, if a man says he has faith but has not works? Can his faith save him? If a brother or sister is ill-clad and in lack of daily food, and one of you says to them, 'Go in peace, be warmed and filled,' without giving them the things needed for the body, what does it profit? So faith by itself, if it has no works, is dead" (James 1:22; 2:14-17).

The Sermon on the Mount (Matthew 5-7) stresses motives and is emphatic on a life that manifests godly fruits. Jesus said, "Let your light so shine before men, that they may see your good works and give glory to your Father who is in heaven" (Matthew 5:16).

Jesus taught his disciples to pray that God's "kingdom come" and his "will be done on earth as it is in heaven." Genuine love of God can only mean growing in obedient love to his will on the earth. Here is where people live, and care should be taken lest religious devotion become a ceremony that has no connection with the will of God in the actual lives of human beings on this earth. The nature of God and his relation to his earth-people determine the way men pray and how they worship him.

THE LEARNER THINKS ABOUT GOD

It is important for the church school teacher to encourage clear study and thinking and questioning about God so that children and youth can grow to accept him and his will. Here follow excerpts that summarize the views of three class-groups.

GOD AS CREATOR
(Fourth Grade)

What is God like?

God was in the beginning.
Look at the world he created and is creating.
The earth rotates around the sun,
The moon gives light at night,
It has always been so.

We stand under the sky,
The stars are in their places making the same patterns.
There is the North Star, the Big Dipper, Orion and Cassiopeia.
The seasons follow in the same order —
Summer, Autumn, Winter, and Spring.

What is God like?

His world runs according to law.
Trees grow on the hillsides.
They take up moisture from the soil.
It always happens that way.
If many trees are cut, the water is uncontrolled.
Then rivers overflow their banks,
Waters flood the land.
The earth provides enough food for all people.
Some nations want more than their share.
Friendships are broken and enemies are made.

What is God like?

God created all life according to a wonderful plan.
Look at yourself.
Are you not wonderfully made?
You can run and jump, you can think, laugh, feel, and talk,
You are alive!
Look at the rest of life in God's world. Is it not wonderful?
The bird who knows when to fly south from the cold;
The animal who crawls into his den;
The tree that drops seeds into the earth.
The beginning of all life was a tiny cell that moved.

What is God like?

2000 years ago a man lived in Palestine.
He had love in his heart.
He told men about a kingdom of God where love rules.
In this kingdom people forgive each other,
They share and are kind.
All men are brothers and God is their Father.
He told us that God is love
And that love must rule in our hearts instead of hate and fear.

God was working in Jesus

God was in the beginning,
God created and is creating life,

God is a spirit. He is with us every day —
God is forever and ever.

WE FIND GOD
(Fifth Grade)

We find God
    In the round white moon that gleams at night
    In the twinkling stars that are so bright,
    In the golden sun that shines all day,
    In the planets that move in an orderly way,
      Millions and millions of miles away.
    In the swaying trees that are so tall
    In their boughs the birds do call,
    In our gardens where seeds we sow,
    In shady forests where wild-flowers grow.
      We find God in all beautiful things.

We find God
    In the waves that break on the sandy shore,
    In the tide that goes out and comes in once more,
    In the morning change from darkness to light,
    In the change from lightness to dark at night,
    In the clouds that hold water till it falls as rain,
    In the brilliant sun that always shines again,
      We find God in all things that go on and on.

We find God
    In Jesus whose love was so perfect and great
    It was given to all and never changed to hate,
    In Jesus whose love was so powerful and strong
    It changed people's lives when they had done wrong;
    His love was like God's, it could not die then
    It has lived on in the hearts of men.
      We find God in all goodness, all kindness and love.[2]

GOD AS CREATOR
(Ninth Grade)

Everything in God's universe is unified
As if it were perfectly planned.
You can compare the smallest conceivable matter
With the largest conceivable mass in the universe,
For in the atom you have particles revolving around a center
Just as our own solar system revolves around a center,

[2] Used by permission of the late Phyllis N. Maramarco.

And all other systems operate on a similar plan.
The balance in each one must be perfect,
Else disastrous things could happen to other systems.
If there were an unbalanced amount of particles in the atom,
Much the same result would take place.
The farther we go into space the more we learn
Of cosmic rays and radiation, meteorology, astronomy,
And many other forms of science.
The more we know, the more we are convinced
There is infinitely more to learn.
All this exploration into space could lead man
Into a better way of life,
As when atoms and isotopes are used in medicine
And the purification of drugs and foods.
It may be possible for man to control the weather
In such ways as making rain,
Or changing the course of a hurricane.
Man can use these forces in two ways,
Either for the good or ill of mankind:
Atoms may be used in medical research,
Or in the atomic bomb;
Control of weather may benefit crops,
Or it may be used in war for destruction of crops;
Control of space might lead to military outposts as a threat to peace,
Or as new frontiers for research and exploration.
We look to God for guidance to use all the sciences rightly.
Scientists must have a faith that drives them on to do research,
A faith that God will help them achieve their goal
For a better way of life.
The Bible says, "In the beginning
God created the heavens and the earth."
Though these words were written twenty-five hundred years ago,
Their basic truth still holds.
The more we probe, the more this belief is strengthened.
Primitive man used to attribute natural forces to superstition.
Now we know the scientific reasons for these forces;
We attribute the organized plan to the continuation of God's creation.
In the beginning God —
God started the process of creation,
And this process still goes on throughout the universe.[3]

3 *Ibid.*

3.
Some Ways to
Learn to Worship

THERE ARE MANY STAGES AND TYPES OF EXPERIENCE that may lead young people and children to genuine Christian worship. In this chapter we shall be looking at a few of these.

THE ROLE OF ADULTS

Children and young people learn much from associating with adults and observing them. It is possible to have an occasional half-hour family worship service in the church sanctuary, where children may observe their parents and other adults reverently participate. This experience, of course, should not be a substitute for worship services graded to their own capacities and needs, or for special worship education in every grade. The young can learn much by experiencing prayer at the table when it is offered in a meaningful way by parents and adults. Rufus Jones wrote in *Finding the Trail of Life:*

> God was just as real a being to me all through my early boyhood as was any one of the persons in our nearest neighbor's house. At home He was talked with every morning, and spoken of all day in a variety of ways. If any sort of crisis was near us His

33

help was asked, in as simple and confident a way as we asked a neighbor's help when we needed it.[1]

A turning point, he says, came when he had gone a step farther than usual, had done something which grieved everybody at home and he "expected a severe punishment, which was administered with extreme infrequency."

> To my surprise my mother took me by the hand and led me to my room; then she solemnly kneeled down by me, and offered a prayer which reached the very inmost soul of me. No holy of holies would ever have seemed to the pious Jew more awful with the presence of God than that chamber seemed to me.[2]

This experience he added, dated an advance upward in his religious life.

Somewhere a Christian mother declared that adults can "use things to *express* their love to their children." She said, "I use a birthday cake as a gift of love. When I serve bacon, eggs, and peanut butter sandwiches, we offer them as a gift to God, for use in our relationships with our children." As parents seek forgiveness of their children, they are witnessing to God's love. In health and in safety for young folks, it may be a part of the dedication of the adult to God's plan and young folks can see this.[3]

TRAINED LEADERSHIP

In the church school, there is need for trained, mature and devoted religious people to lead and to guide children in worship. Their respect for the children themselves will be of primary consideration as with devotion and intelligence they

---

1 *Finding the Trail of Life,* by Rufus M. Jones (New York: The Macmillan Company, 1926), p. 102. Used by permission of Girard Trust Bank, Philadelphia. Inspiring help for parents and teachers who are aiding young people to know God.

2 *Ibid.,* p. 109.

3 See *Man's Need and God's Action,* by Reuel L. Howe (New York: Seabury Press, 1953). Unusual and valuable guidance in the religious meaning of relationship.

help these young students to grow in worshiping. To be helpful, such leaders must be prepared in numerous aspects of worship:

Why we worship

The nature of God

The beginnings of children's comprehension of God

How man can relate his life and daily activities to God's will and order

The nature of prayer

How to pray at different age-levels and on varied occasions

Appropriate hymns and music for the age levels being led in worship

How to create services of worship

Suitable themes for the worship of particular ages

How to select stories and data for the "concreteness" in the worship service

How to tell stories

How to use Scripture in worship

How to motivate, to take up, and to receive the offering

HOW SOME YOUNG FOLKS LEARNED

A new teacher, on his first day in the church school, discovered that something was wrong. His senior high boys straggled into the crowded church indifferently while the superintendent managed the "opening exercises." The boys appeared bored. Their conversation reflected how far removed was their attention from the service that was being conducted. When the class met, the teacher began to question himself about the needs of these boys. What could he do with such an active group of boys? Had he anything to offer? While he was rapidly searching his own mind, he overheard a criticism of the superintendent. He listened and then asked, "Why is it you do not like the service?" Comments came quick and fast. The teacher's question was like opening the gates of a dam. In a stream the criticisms rushed forth until the teacher knew his textbook need not concern him for a while. He noted such criticisms as:

"The service is not interesting."

"There is no order to the service."

"They don't try to keep it quiet."

"They never ask any of the pupils to take part."

"What's the use of worship?"

"The superintendent talks too much."

"Who wants to listen to a long, dry talk?"

"We don't have any time left for class discussion."

The teacher continued to listen until the boys seemed aware of his full interest, and then he asked, "What do you think we should do about it?" A few suggestions followed:

"The programs could be more varied."

"Some of the pupils could take part."

"The service should be shorter."

"There could be ushers so that the program would not be interrupted."

"Little children ought to have a place by themselves."

The teacher pressed the question further. "Can we do anything about this situation?" It seemed to surprise the boys to think that *they* might do something. Perhaps it was the optimistic attitude of the teacher that lured them on; but, whatever the cause, by the close of their brief class period they had decided not to "take up the book" until later on and to think further about worship in their church school.

The teacher was challenged. He had never led services of worship, and he had never studied about the subject. But early in the week he sought an interview with an experienced Christian educator to get some help. They discussed worship in the church school, and he decided to make available for his class some varied materials and to begin a serious study of the matter. These materials became the reference library for reports and plans. An interview with the minister and the superintendent provided the cooperation necessary to begin such an original adventure in this church school. The boys rapidly became engrossed in their subject. They discovered that they knew very little about worship and worship services and admitted that they would have to study the subject more thoroughly before they could expect to change their own school. During the following weeks the boys began talking with their parents, their friends, and their minister about worship. One boy took notes on a radio lecture on worship and reported to the class.

The reference material selected by the teacher became more and more popular as the subject became better organized for study. A "Test of Religious Thinking" (advanced), then published by the Association Press, New York (1945), opened up numerous questions that occupied the interest of the boys for several sessions. It also served as an excellent guide for the teacher in locating the problems in the religious concepts of the boys.

After a few weeks the class was invited to present the students' recommendations for church school worship to the teachers of the whole school. This proved to be a great challenge to the boys. They wanted to do it well and to know what they were doing. Now they found that Sunday sessions were too short, so they sought out their teacher for extra sessions. They began to investigate what other church schools were doing. They read and discussed at length.

After several weeks of self-imposed research the group of rugged high-school boys sat down for the first time with the church school leaders in conference together. In earnest fashion they offered their report. The adult leaders were keenly interested and asked many questions. On that evening the following recommendations were adopted:

1. That the worship service be limited to fifteen minutes and more time be given to the classes.

2. That worship come at the close of the morning class sessions.

3. That talks be shorter and that stories be more frequently substituted and given by different young people.

4. That the service be more carefully planned and more formal.

5. That measures be taken to prevent confusion and disturbance during the sessions; that there be ushers.

6. That the worship be graded and that there be several separate worship groups.

7. That a representative of the boys' class be chosen as a permanent member of the church school board.

Finally the teachers asked the boys if they would not lead a service as a demonstration for the church school. This request was taken up at the next class session and accepted as their next job, on condition that they be allowed ample time to prepare the service.

There was eagerness to get to work and a midweek meeting of the class became a necessity. The teacher worked with the pastor and the superintendent in order to pave the way for the coming worship service and its results. The boys worked diligently for weeks on their service. Committees were appointed to make reports on different phases of the worship service. In choosing hymns they found themselves involved in the discussion of music, ideas of God, of Jesus, and the social ideals in the hymns. A prelude was found with the assistance of the church organist. They carefully considered the atmosphere of the room in order to help people to worship during the "quiet music" and other parts of the service.

A prayer was prepared by the class after considerable thought had been given to the subject of prayer in general and its place in the worship service. And so this teacher taught this class to pray.

Finally, their first service for the church school was ready. Every detail in the program had been carefully studied and considerable attention given to the general atmosphere of the room in which the service was held. The sincerity and interest of the boys as they led the service convinced many of the adult leaders that they were offering a better way to worship than this church school had been experiencing. Slowly the teachers began to make changes. The young children were given rooms for their own program and finally the young people succeeded in having their service in the worshipful new church auditorium. A council made up of representatives from the different classes assumed responsibility for the services of worship. Much guidance and leadership for this new departure came from the boys who had learned something about worship and how to plan services.

The climax of the boys' adventure in worship seemed to come when they were asked to plan and to direct a dedication of one of the new rooms in their church. In the past months they had accumulated background and sources of material. The results of their weeks of work came to light. A beautiful service built around the theme "A Quest for God" helped the large assembly of people to realize how varied and many have been the ways by which men have come to know God. Through special music, hymns, poetry, original presentations of biblical worship, and prayer, this group of high school youth prepared the congregation for the dedication of their new hall.

A teacher whose group had been characterized as "trouble makers" had thus used a situation full of conflict and turned it into an educational triumph. He had respected the opinions of his boys and was able to join them in learning much about worship and more about worship procedures for their own church school. As a result he had succeeded in developing a more intelligent leadership that promised much for the future of this church.

Situations Leading to Prayer

Classes may be working on problems and questions that lead into the creation of poems, litanies, prayers, and hymns.

A snowfall, an ice storm, a change of seasons, the emergence of a moth or butterfly from a cocoon, and numerous other happenings may require a teacher to change his plans and in them. Out of these a prayer of praise may originate and develop.[4]

A tragedy may be known to all in the class, such as some miners trapped underground, or a motor car accident, or a plane crash, or an epidemic, or some heroic failure—all of these and others may become the focus of attention in almost any class of older children or young people. A suitable discussion could lead to the creation of a relevant prayer—either by the group thinking together or by individuals writing prayers after some thinking has been done.

Such questions as these may aid in teaching young folks to pray:

Will God change his laws of the universe if we ask him?

How much does God depend on people to learn to use his laws for good? To make the world more beautiful? To make life happier and more safe and healthful for people?

In what ways do people need to learn more about God's ways of working in the world?

If we were working with God, what would we do about our treatment of people of other races or religions?

What would we do about war?

What would we do about people who are underfed or uneducated in providing for life today?

Such experiences as these may lead to worship or to the creation of hymns and prayers:

1. Reading poems and Psalms about God and thinking over the ideas in them.

2. Comparing ideas of God as found in different periods in the Bible. See *How Our Religion Began*, by Edna M. Baxter (New York: Harper & Row, 1939).

4 See prayers in Chapter 19, for example.

3. Making slides or posters to show the varied ways the Hebrews of the Bible worshiped God.

4. Watching a snowstorm and catching snow crystals on dark cloth or paper; making varied paper ones.

TRAINING SESSIONS

A period of time in the Sunday church school, in the vacation school, or in the camp, needs to be set aside for learning the meaning and procedures of worship, studying the significance of gifts for God's work, and becoming familiar with the hymns and responses useful for each age in its worship.

The first step in learning to worship in formal situations involves practices and habits that make the service run along smoothly. If a class is to use a processional to go to a particular place in a room, or to a chapel, this must be rehearsed until children learn to walk and to sing in orderly fashion as they go to their seats.

Usually the worshipers rise on the last bar of the accompanist's introduction and start singing when a characteristic chord is struck. Older children can learn to sing the "Amen" at the close of hymns.

Some churches have particular attitudes and postures for praying: kneeling, extending the arms, bowing the heads, closing the eyes. The leader will interpret the history or the meaning of these forms. He will explain that closing the eyes shuts out distractions so that the worshiper may concentrate on God and on what is being said to God.

Children can learn when to stand for a hymn or a response and when to sit down. Whatever order is used in the service should be more or less permanent in the church school. Details about taking up the offering will require rehearsal and interpretation.

Training in worship should be distinct from the formal

service of worship, yet always be done reverently and religiously.

People of all ages need time to discuss the problems which may arise out of their experiences in worship. Often these involve questions about God and his nature. Teen-agers may need to learn something of the changing practices of worship recorded in the Bible and the struggles of Protestants in their attempt to overcome meaningless forms and ceremony. They may be interested in the growth of Quaker worship and its meaning. In addition to a worship training period, there is a need for fully developed courses to study worship.

Third- or fourth-grade children may study *Tell Me About Prayer* by Mary Alice Jones (Chicago: Rand McNally & Co., 1948), and learn to create their own prayers for varied occasions. Sixth- or seventh-grade students may have a long course on the varied conceptions of God and his worship in the Old Testament. *How Our Religion Began* by the author (*op. cit.*) is suggestive. Adolescents need a course in prayer, using such a book as *More Than We Are* by Margueritte H. Bro (New York: Harper & Row, 1948) and *I Believe* by Nevin C. Harner (Philadelphia: United Church Press, 1950).

Children and young people in the church school should be learning continuously a rich and suitable repertoire of hymns and responses. These should be taught well in advance of their use in the formal services in the elementary and upper-grade worship. Camps, vacation schools, and Sunday sessions should work together to create a rich background of worship resources and education. Sometimes order and behavior in worship will require attention and discussion.

Thought may be given to the seating and the arrangement of the room for worship so that all can see, hear, and participate properly in the service.

Much of the Scripture for worship suggested in this book may involve memorization and oral or unison use. Some occasions may require choric reading of biblical materials. All of these uses of the Bible involve practice. Examples are given in Part II.

Not the least effective procedure in learning to worship is the act of worship itself, either in a service or on informal occasions when one becomes aware of God or is inspired by God to do something. A discovery, a sense of mystery when children see a moth emerge from a cocoon, when they examine blood, when they right a wrong, when they plan for the comfort or well-being of a group or an individual—all of these and many more may provide moments of worship because a fuller consciousness of God has dawned.

Adolescents are frequently expected to lead services of worship, but too rarely do they have adequate study and guidance in significant procedures and in the meaning of what they are doing. Their motives may be satisfaction in standing before a group, being called on to do something in their group, or feeling that they must have their turn. The wise leader can use these motives and guide the young people to find richer meanings.

A church school class or youth group could well spend time over a period of several months in carrying out a practical study of worship. While preparing services they may learn more about God and how people can have a relationship to him; they may examine hymns for concepts and ideas and make a list of worthy hymns to be used (such as those in Chapter 17 of this book). They could study prayer by the help of such a book as *Prayer and the Common Life* by Georgia E. Harkness (Nashville: Abington Press, 1948) and search for significant prayers as found in *More Than We Are* by Margueritte H. Bro (*op. cit.*). They could create prayers for varied occasions. The order and arrangement of the services also involve study and thought.

Basic in their growth in worship must be the knowledge of God and provision for his will and spirit to rule and to teach.

Recognition of the Students' Perspective

Ultimately the basic concern in the preparation of young folks to worship God may be stated in terms of understanding and sharing creatively God's purposes. The aspiration one feels when one is moved to be a better person is just one aspect of the worship experience.

For children to grow in worship involves an ever-widening concept of God's purposes. Can their leaders relate the purposes of God to the daily realm of children and their groups?

Much of the training in worship becomes valuable because cumulatively the varied aspects of these experiences grow to be enriching. They take on increased value as insight and practice deepen and broaden.

The universe of the child is generally far less broad than that of the adult. The child has to be led to greater heights and vision to have more and more of God's perspective. The outlook from the child's experiences needs to be evaluated and examined continuously, from God's perspective. By his spirit of love an ever-widening appreciation of his purposes for people will make worship fruitful.

Adults need constantly to be reminded that mere quiet and form are not the ultimate test of worship but rather an inner condition and change in the attitudes and spirit of children. They can grow "in spirit and in truth."

"Even a child makes himself known by his acts, whether what he does is pure and right" (Proverbs 20:11).

4.
The Formal
Worship Setting

THE PLACE OF FORMAL WORSHIP needs to be planned so that the worshiper can think about God and his purposes. So far as possible, there should be no distractions, no disorderly or confusing conditions. The setting should be clean and beautiful even though it may be very simple. The worshiper should face an uncluttered wall free from wraps and unsightly materials.

WORSHIP CENTERS

Worship centers should also be free from clutter. Inappropriate settings may better give way to none at all. Taste and suitability are not always understood by leaders of worship. What we see when we gather as a group for worship can be very important. It should be suggestive of worship as well as beauty and dignity.

Children under six years of age do well to gather informally into a "huddle" around a teacher in an intimate, friendly grouping, perhaps seated on a rug. Usually, children are above three years of age before they can sit down in a group for even a few minutes. A low table, near the teacher, may contain flowers or colored leaves or growing bulbs or other pertinent objects, but never a confusion of things. Back of the table may be a lovely large nature picture well mounted, or the Cizek picture of Jesus and the children referred to later in this chapter.

By the six- or seven-year age, and continuously through adolescence, there can be a more formal center of worship. Some liturgical churches will have an altar and others, less liturgical, a communion table. In most, there will be a table and a desk or lectern for the leader. There should be two chairs, one at each side of the table.

If it is possible to have graded worship, there may be a built-in worship center in the individual room covered by doors which open at each side, like a triptych, to reveal it for use when the class is ready for worship. This worship center may be recessed into the wall and yet not be very deep. Here the doors will be painted so as to focus on the center, where there may be candles, offering plates, and perhaps a picture or mural or a carving or just a lovely dossal curtain against the wall.

Symbols are abstract and not expressive to young children. By adolescent age, however, the cross may become meaningful to them. Tall wrought-iron candlesticks may be placed at the ends of the table, giving it a frame of light.

Doubtless Quaker groups will prefer an undecorated and plain wall for meditation and thinking. Some groups use a fireplace as the center.

When the worship center is more formal, a tall, wide, plain dossal curtain without design or pattern is effective. Usually it needs to be lined if it is to hang well, and it must be wide enough to hang full from a wrought-iron rod. It needs to look substantial and impressive. In some rooms it should hang from the ceiling level.

Though adults in some communions will be concerned about the liturgical symbolism of colors selected for worship centers, the symbolic element is minimized with children. Here the main consideration is suitability for the room and the age of the worshipers. Green is a safe color for the dossal curtains. For young children, a golden velvet is effective. Dark red is better for older ages and in large rooms.

The table [1] may not need a covering if it is simple and of good construction. If it is covered, however, the same material should be used as for the dossal curtain. When the table is a symbol of the communion, it is covered for that service only.

If candles are used, it is customary for them to be white. In the beginning they were doubtless needed for light, but gradually they assumed symbolic meaning: two candles representing the human and the divine nature of Christ. Protestants, however, need not use candles for their worship. Liturgical and orthodox churches have very particular symbolic uses for candles.

It is well today to note the problem of symbolism in the church of the Middle Ages and heed its difficulties. "Symbolism (so far as it was to be found in the village church) no doubt tried to meet the needs of the illiterate, but symbolism was a very vague and unsettled method of communication and gave rise to innumerable errors and rash speculations," writes H. S. Bennett in *Life on the English Manor*.[2]

PLACE OF WORSHIP

Chapels are expensive and unfortunately can only be used by scheduling age groups at awkward times in the program of teaching. Though they will serve for weddings and funerals and special services, they hardly meet the needs of a large church school. In general, graded worship arrangements may

[1] For adult practices see *The Arts of the Church,* by Richard H. Ritter (Boston: Pilgrim Press, 1947), p. 52.

[2] *A Study of Peasant Conditions, 1150-1400* (New York: Cambridge University Press, 1960), p. 32. Used by permission.

give better training in worship than mass meetings of too varied age groups of children in a chapel.

There are many crowded church schools with few provisions for worship. Adjustments can be made, however. For instance, if the children are meeting in an assembly hall or a gymnasium, large panel-type screens (approximately six feet high and eight feet long) may be made to wheel into place for an enclosure. One of these may have a dossal curtain hung from the top, serving as the background for a table, lectern, and chairs.

The out-of-doors can provide lovely and inspiring worship settings. A backdrop of interlaced branches of trees with a rough-hewn table and lectern may be created in a camp or beside a rural church and be used for older children, young people, and adults for varied services. Such a setting would be most desirable for vacation-school worship. Sometimes adolescent groups create such out-of-door worship places themselves.

PICTURES FOR WORSHIP CENTERS

Pictures, if they are appropriate and well mounted or framed, may serve as the focus for the young worshipers. A large permanent picture frame may be adapted by putting a hinged plywood back on it, which enables the leader to open it and change pictures easily, using a standard size of mounting board which fits the frame.

For the nursery and kindergarten rooms the author has found that "Jesus and the Children" by Bella Vichon of the Cizek School is one of the simplest and best of the religious pictures. At the older age levels, some of Elsie Anna Wood's large, colorful pictures are useful. Mounted on a wide gold mat, they appear especially significant and beautiful.

At Christmas time "The First Flower Service," by Margaret Tarrant, seems simplest for kindergarten children. "Suffer Little Children to Come unto Me" is useful on occasions of worship with primary children, in thinking of Jesus' teachings about how to treat people. "He Taught Them" can be relevant in most Christian emphases with older ages and will be useful when Christian teachings are used to follow the story or talk. This can become one of the more permanent pictures in older children's worship.

For older children, at the Christmas season, Elsie Anna Wood's "Glory to God in the Highest, and on Earth Peace" will be useful. "Hilltop at Nazareth," by the same artist, is a delightful picture of the boy Jesus overlooking Nazareth and surrounded by flowers of the field, mountains and sky.

For adolescent worship, there are several pictures which may be used more or less continuously. Certainly Elsie Anna Wood's "He Taught Them" can be used. Others are "The Presence," A. E. Borthwick; "The Commission," Eugene Burnand; "Go Preach," Eugene Burnand; "Omnipresent," Rosenkranz; and "Christ and the Fishermen," Zimmerman.

THE SYMBOL

In general a symbol is a material or concrete object designed to represent an immaterial or abstract idea. Thus it becomes a help in understanding when used at an age level at which the idea symbolized can be comprehended and when the person himself is not too literal-minded to miss the symbolic interpretation. Symbols which are too advanced for a child to grasp are apt to be for him mere form or mere decoration. Too much abstraction dulls interest and significance for the young worshiper.

Symbols have developed out of the life of the growing, changing church, and once served particularly the illiterate. About the fourth century the cross became popular. About the time Constantine made Christianity the official religion of the empire, the cross appeared on the banners of some of his soldiers.

Because the cross (especially the crucifix, which ceases to be a symbol and becomes representative art) has bulked so large in Roman Catholic art, Protestants have tended to neglect it. Among all the symbols, however, the cross seems to be the most basic for the Christian. It stands for a way of life of one who "humbled himself and became obedient unto death, even death on a cross" (Philippians 2:8). It symbolizes sacrificial service carried on to the point of laying down his life for his beliefs and for his friends.

When the whole life of Jesus can be properly studied and appreciated, the proper time has come to introduce this significant symbol of the cross. The child would not be younger than the fifth- or sixth-grade level, and perhaps more wisely the seventh-grade level, before an abstract symbol of such importance is used.

The Episcopal church has published a resource book for adolescents to use somewhat as a dictionary, *More Than Words*, (New York: Seabury Press, Inc., 1955). It clearly interprets, many religious terms and symbols and should be most helpful in a liturgical church. Other denominations will also find it useful in their work with adolescents.

One of the common symbols in the Christian church is some form of the Lord's Supper. It has a long history and represents the beloved community at a common table. Its interpretation has varied, but it has retained a unique sign of sacredness. Such a symbol demands maturity before it can have significance. The worshiper taking communion needs to understand the life of Jesus and its meaning as well as something of the history of the Christian movement. Adolescents are considered by many leaders to be as young as communion participants should be.

By ninth grade, young people are likely to have studied the history of the Christian movement and to have learned something of Christian symbols. Therefore, by this time, many of these symbols may have real meaning for them. In particular, any symbols that appear frequently in their own church should be studied and understood by adolescents. They can create a booklet from time to time to interpret important symbols in the windows, the frescoes, the altar, the communion table, the vestments, and in the architecture. To become significant, some history behind these symbols should be known. Workers with youth will be inspired by L. A. Convis' *Adventuring into the Church* (New York: Harper & Row, 1951), which is a program for preparing young people for church membership. A graphic and interesting book by Friedrich Rest, *Our Christian Symbols* (Philadelphia: Christian Education Press, 1954) will be another useful reference, as will *Religious Symbolism* by F. Ernest Johnson (New York: Harper & Row, 1955).

5.
Themes for Worship

THEMES FOR PREPARED WORSHIP SERVICES grow out of the meaning of God and his revelation as well as his relation to every form of life associated with the experiences of people on the earth. Awareness of God and his will in everything that happens requires thoughtful meditation. Scripture, experiences of other people, hymns, and prayers can encourage such attention. God is seeking his people but he leaves them free to respond or not. Thus worship becomes a form of glad and willing response to God's invitation as people learn to grow in friendship and love for God. The practice of his presence, thinking his thoughts, abiding by his spirit, loving him, requires time, effort, and earnest consideration and devotion.

Planned worship experiences ought to emphasize and stimulate an awareness of God's relation to all of life and to his will as supreme in all of man's decisions and activities. One realm after another should come under the testing of God's will and spirit. Children and young people respond better when worship services relate their understanding of God to *concrete* aspects of life where they are living it. Abstract subjects dealing with generalizations, object lessons, or with symbolic experiments and stories may be entertaining but ineffective for genuine results in worship. The talk or story needs to be grounded in a situation, a problem, an event, or a struggle, close to the needs and feelings of the listener's age and life situation. After such concreteness may follow Scripture which sharpens the Christian insight, and then prayer to express appreciation, thanksgiving, aspiration, evaluation of behavior, repentance, or dedication. For younger children the climax in prayer may well be appreciation and thanksgiving.[1]

There are many concrete areas of life in the church and in the lives of its children and young people that should be faced by them in worship as coming under the rule of God.

WHEN GIVING SERVICE OR GIFTS

The motivation of service and of giving for Christian purposes may well constitute the theme and content of a series of services for older children and young people.

One group of juniors was planning to give gifts to children in an institution at Christmas time. The director of religious education went to the institution, gathered factual data about its children, and then wrote stories which enabled her juniors to respect, understand, and wish to show friendship to them at Christmas time. Such a plan might be followed with regard to people in institutions for the blind, for crippled children, for the aged, for the mentally ill, for the mentally retarded, or for children from broken homes.

A series of worship services for second- and third-graders was developed around the area of life of orphan children in Korea, because they had a Korean woman in charge of their worship who made her faraway country a reality to them as she told stories of the orphans.

[1] See Chapter 7 for the order of prepared services.

EVALUATION OF SOCIAL PRACTICES

The worshiper ought to face various personal and social practices in life around him, and evaluate these according to God's spirit of love and righteousness. These situations may involve the following:

Racial events (both good and bad)

Labor and workers (migrants, unhealthy and dangerous places to work, careless workmanship, great devotion to duty and responsibility)

New residential construction or renovation in place of slums

Family living

Better health for masses of people

Use of science for the service of mankind

Play and leisure-time living

In services built around such data the Christian needs to feel stimulated to work for the welfare of people as members of God's family. The worshiper ought to grow in his concern for ever-wider areas of living, always considering the improvement of his own relationships to God's purposes in life where he lives it.

APPRECIATION OF GOD'S GIFTS

Another realm for worship lies in the individual's awareness of the gifts coming to him from other peoples of many types, the sacrifice of some for the welfare of all, and the beauty and majesty of God's creation. Such services may lead to appreciation, thanksgiving, and praise. They may include vivid, dramatic portrayals of the varied work done to clothe, to feed, and to house people. Stories may be told of people who have labored, studied, and even risked their lives for scientific discoveries to improve man's living. The emphasis should be on service and on a contribution to life rather than on attempts to be heroic. Heroism, as such, may not be a suitable goal for a Christian, but activities of men and women struggling to gain peace and brotherhood are truly significant.

CHILDREN'S QUESTIONS AND PROBLEMS ABOUT GOD

In Helen Parkhurst's interviews, a typical child's response was, "I've always been puzzled about Him [God]. People say He is everywhere, but airplanes have been flying pretty high and they haven't come across Him."

Another child declared, "My mother and father told me about Him and I thought He . . . could do most anything. When I did anything wrong I was taught that God was supposed to fix everything . . . . When sometimes I got a severe punishment, that shattered my belief in Him."

Another child responded by saying, "Yes, my ideas of God have changed terribly, because of all the problems in my life. I started out with a sincere belief in Him, and it was considerably shaken by . . . oh, lots of things." [2]

FACING CHILDREN'S QUESTIONS

Life, birth, death, failure, disaster all involve children (as well as adults) in numerous religious questions. For example, does God plan hurricanes, storms, and sickness to punish people? A young child says, "I hate God. He killed my friend."

In one fourth grade the following questions emerged:

Were the Indians once the only people on earth?
Is the story of Adam and Eve right or is science right?
Is the Bible true?
Does God punish us by sending hurricanes, storms, and sickness?
Why do people have to die?

Some primary children reflect their confusion about the relation of God to life:

Can God see me? Can he see me down in the basement? Can he see me if I cover myself all up with the blankets?
How can God be with daddy in New York and be here too?

2 *Exploring the Child's World,* by Helen Parkhurst (New York: Appleton-Century, 1951), pp. 213, 214, 215. Used by permission.

I hate God. He let my puppy get run over.
I don't believe in God. I prayed every night for a bicycle and
he didn't give it to me.
Where is God?
Doesn't God love the children in Greece? Why does he let them
starve?
Is God as nice as you?

In a ninth-grade class, the following questions were asked:

Was God ever on earth?
Do you think God was a real man?
Is God personal or impersonal?
How do you distinguish God from Jesus?
Does God punish you for doing wrong?
How does God work through the church?
Will God always rule, or will something else take his place?
Is God all-powerful?
Why is there evil if God is love?
Is Christianity the only *right* religion?
Does God *create* life after death?
What happens after people die?
How does prayer help us to learn the will of God?
What is God like?

Services may be built around such children's and young
people's questions as: Who and where is God? Does he love
good people better than bad people? Where do we go when
we die? Where did we come from? How was the earth made?
Such questions cannot be answered glibly but will require
leaders who can think clearly, honestly, and with feeling and
sincerity. There will be a sharing as in a search. These
themes will require several sessions. Perhaps such a book as
Margueritte H. Bro's *When Children Ask* (New York: Harper & Row, 1956) will stimulate an awareness of suitable
themes for worship.

There are themes which may give vision to young folks
about the unseen realities in the universe, such as the examination of feelings. Love feelings may be contrasted and
compared with feelings of hate. How we feel when we have

concern for the needs of other people. How we feel when we really try to share or help other people. For young people's services, ideas may be developed from *Why Should I?* by Ellen Walpole (New York: Harper & Row, 1949).

Such a general theme as "Understanding God" may lead into the problems and questions of older children. What is God's place in the seasons, the rain and storms and floods, the growth of plants and animals, or the failures in their development? Will God stop the rain for an individual who asks him? If God is kind and loving, why are people injured and killed in storms and earthquakes? What is man's part and what is God's part in airplane tragedies and automobile accidents? How much does God depend on people to keep us well? What is God's part? In what ways do people need to learn more about God's ways of working in the world?

Special Days

Special days in the calendar of the church or nation will provide occasions for celebration in worship and frequently require a whole series of services. Thanksgiving, Christmas, and Easter will be particularly important for themes. On the child's level, the leader may derive much help from *Thoughts of God for Boys and Girls* by Edith Frances Welker and Aimee A. Barber (New York: Harper & Row, 1948), and *As We Think with God* by Phyllis N. Maramarco and Edith Frances Welker, eds. (Nashville: Abingdon Press, 1962).

Suggestive Themes

Each formal service of worship in the school of the church — weekday, vacation, or Sunday — is usually fifteen or twenty minutes in length. It is important that themes be carried on over a period of time, generally about six weeks; for example, a series on "Workers Who Feed Us" leading to Thanksgiving or a series leading up to Easter, "Goodness Lives On and On in People." The concrete aspect of the service can be presented in talks or through properly prepared stories. The Scripture follows the story or talk and may be read from a poster or recited in choric fashion from memory. The same Bible passage may well be used for the whole series on a given theme. It is followed by a climax prayer.

Build themes around specific data reflecting *particular* concrete aspects of goodness, truth, and beauty which reflect religious meaning for the worshipers. Use these concrete materials to lead to prayers of appreciation and hymns of praise. Stimulate gratitude and a recognition of the place of God in the depth of each of these realms. Avoid abstraction and symbolism as far as possible. The following are some possible lines of development:

1. God's rule is dependable
   A. How can man rely on God in the realm of health?
      (1) Consider research people
      (2) Consider the doctors serving people, apart from the motive of fees
      (3) Consider the importance of taking God's truth in medicine to needy people in America and in other parts of the world. Note Dr. Albert Schweitzer and Dr. Thomas Dooley
   B. Emphasize the cooperation of men in brotherhood and love in using God's order to serve people in such a realm as health and disease or in the instance of hunger and the use of technical knowledge to create more good. Note the work of agricultural missions
   C. See mental health in relation to God's order. What a man thinks affects his body and his behavior
   D. See the rule of love as a very fundamental law of the universe. "Where love is absent there is separation and self-isolation that is the essence of sin"
      (1) In the family
      (2) In friendships
      (3) In race relations

    (4) In labor and industry
    (5) In interfaith relations
    (6) In community affairs
    (7) As a member of the church

2. Our lives belong to God and only become whole when we work with him in love and in following his order
   A. What to do to overcome our self-centered or ego-centered living?
   B. How to work with God in school? (worry, study, purpose)
   C. How to work with God in relation to human need
   D. How to work with God in the family

3. What does God require of us in relation to:
   A. The American Indians
   B. The Jews
   C. The Negroes
   D. The Chinese
   E. The Russians

4. What is the meaning for us of being "servants" as Jesus taught it to his disciples at the Last Supper?

5. The power of goodness on God's terms never dies. Its continuing effects may be seen in the following:
   A. Jesus
   B. The growth of Jesus' spirit in the Roman Empire
   C. George Fox and some of his followers
   D. William Penn and modern leaders of reconciliation
   E. A family

6. How to work on God's terms
   A. As a laborer
   B. As an employer
   C. As a doctor
   D. As a wife
   E. As a father
   F. In cases of wrong; injustice
   G. In school

7. Prophetic implications for modern followers of Jesus. See *Naught for Your Comfort* by Trevor Huddleston (New York: Doubleday, 1956), *Cry the Beloved Country* by Alan Paton (New York: Charles Scribner's Sons, 1950), or the work of Martin Luther King

8. Thanksgiving for some of the many people who feed us. Use talks or data to create sensitivity to our interdependence and our need of brotherhood

9. Services that lead us to evaluate our attitudes and behavior and to change our feelings
    A. How it would feel to be a Negro in America (a series)
    B. How it would feel to be a Jew (a series)
    C. How it would feel to be segregated or badly housed or hungry — dealing with specific peoples (a series)
    D. How it would feel to live in Hungary. See *Toward Morning* by Alta S. Seymour (Chicago: Follett Publishing Co., 1961)

10. God's Love for All People
    A. All colors
    B. The poor
    C. The sinful
    D. Other nations

11. The power of vicarious suffering as seen in specific lives: research people, bringing about changes for the welfare of others in love while meeting opposition; particularly suffering as seen in Jesus

SOME THEMES FOR WORSHIP IN PRIMARY GRADES

1. Varied kinds of people who help to feed us may be described vividly so as to lead to a prayer of thanksgiving for their skills and labor and condition. *God works through people who care for us.* We could arrange a series of services of thanksgiving for the many people involved in giving us milk; or a series on people involved in giving us bread. In

each case we should try to make clear and dramatic our interdependence and the role of God as creator of the laws and the order which we learn to follow.

2. Bringing happiness to some aged people in a home. A series of stories about these people and what our gifts and visits will mean to them may lead to the climax in a trip to one of these homes with our gifts or our program and perhaps a worship service.

3. How God has planned to keep us well. Stories of people involved in this process may include scientists who have carried on research, the role of medical schools, and the work of doctors.

4. A series of services on our fathers, leading to thanksgiving for their work for us.

5. A series of services about the way God works in the world. For help, see *Tell Me About God,* by Mary Alice Jones (Chicago: Rand McNally & Co., 1943), *Thoughts of God for Boys and Girls (op. cit.),* and *As We Think with God (op. cit.).*

6. How we can grow. See *Always Growing,* by Elizabeth Manwell (Boston: Beacon Press, 1957).

7. The true story of lights in the sky. For data see *How Miracles Abound,* by Bertha Stevens (Boston: Beacon Press, 1941), *Beginnings: Earth, Sky, Life, Death,* by Sophia Lyon Fahs and Dorothy T. Spoerl (Boston: Beacon Press, 1958), and *Stars* by Hans A. Rey (Boston: Houghton Mifflin Co., 1961).

8. God's part and man's part in the growth of plants.

THEMES FOR JUNIOR AND JUNIOR HIGH AGES

1. How people have found God. See *How Our Religion Began,* by Edna M. Baxter (New York: Harper & Row, 1939) or *Their Search for God,* by Florence Fitch (New York: Lothrop, Lee & Shepard Co., 1947).

2. Men are of one blood. See *All About Us,* by Eva Knox Evans (New York: Capitol Publishing, 1947) and *People Are*

Important, also by Eva Knox Evans (New York: Capitol Publishing, 1951).

3. How people have helped us to have freedom. See *Lone Journey,* by Jeanette Eaton (New York: Harcourt, Brace & World Inc., 1944).

4. How it must feel to be a migrant. See *Judy's Journey,* by Lois Lenski (New York: Oxford University Press, 1955), and "Living with Others," *Thoughts of God* (op. cit.) Vol. 17, No. 2, 1952.

5. How people have worked for peace. See *Gandhi,* by Jeanette Eaton (New York: Wm. Morrow & Co., 1950).

6. How doctors have worked with God's plan. See *Albert Schweitzer, Genius of the Jungle,* by Joseph Gollomb (New York: Vanguard Press, 1949). Send to the Metropolitan Life Insurance Co., New York City, for their free storybooks on medical researchers or discovers. Consider hospitals in mission lands or the need for medical care in America and other lands.

7. Getting acquainted with a refugee camp or someone else to whom your group is planning to send a gift in empathy and love

8. God as creator: using varied aspects of nature

9. How it would feel to be hungry

10. What it means to work with God

6.
Preparing Services
of Worship

PERHAPS THE FIRST STEP in arranging a service of worship is
to face the fact that God can be worshiped anytime and anywhere, whether it be in a busy street, during an accident, at
the occasion of birth in a hospital, while making a great decision, when righting a wrong, on a mountaintop, beside the
sea, at fellowship with the family, or on any other occasion
where the meaning of God's rule and purpose emerges in the
life of people. Nevertheless, children and youth need to have
a great deal of guidance in their awareness of God as spirit,
his presence in all living, and his purpose in every aspect of
life. Though God can be worshiped anywhere, it is helpful
to plan and create services for particular places and times —
often in the church.

WORSHIP AT THE CLOSE OF A MEETING

More thought needs to be given in our churches to the
effective closing of discussions and work meetings of young
people and adults. Usually at the close of such an experience
minds have been stimulated and there can be a readiness for
repentance, dedication, or thanksgiving and praise. Here is

the occasion for genuine worship, if appropriate provision is made for it, and often it will be much more vital than worship at the opening of a meeting. The traditional opening of the church school and other meetings with "so-called" worship may find the young people and adults cold and unprepared. Such services too often become perfunctory or merely fill in the time while late-comers are arriving!

Informal services at the *close* of Sunday evening fellowship or work sessions, or after discussions or reports in young people's gatherings, will not usually require a sermon, talk, or a story. This may be the time for guided silent meditation, for a litany previously created by a committee and growing out of the group's experiences, or for a carefully planned oral prayer, followed by just the right hymn to gather up the mood of this service. At times the occasion may call for the reading of a mosaic of scripture or of poetry, or for a small dramatic scene followed by silent prayer and a recorded or "live" musical meditation.

There may be a presentation of a living situation, perhaps through a story, film, or role-playing, relevant to what has been discussed in the preceding session. This could be followed by two or three important questions for meditation and silent prayer.

Following some discussions, the group may be stimulated to worship by a careful use of important teachings of the prophets or of Jesus. These can be done in unison reading or given by a verse-speaking choir.

SOME PRINCIPLES IN PREPARING A SERVICE OF WORSHIP

The purpose of the service should be to lead the worshiper to respond to the invitation, "Be still and know that I am God," and to express his sincere devotion to God. Worship services may encourage individuals to dedicate one area of life after another to God's will. Some services will involve the facing of faults in one's personal life or in groups of which one is a part, and the evaluation of these faults in God's presence. There are services which create an awareness of the greatness of God's creation, its order, its beauty and its mystery. Still other services deal with the interdependence of people and God's dependable rule in all aspects of life.

Certain physical and social conditions can aid the worshiper. The room needs to be attractive, orderly, and with a focal point created by a worship center. The seating ought to bring the worshipers together, rather than scattering or dividing them. They need to have appropriately-sized chairs or seats for their own age.

The leaders should be reverent and well prepared. Not only should they be free from coats and hats, but they may under some circumstances wear choir robes or ecclesiastical robes to add dignity to the worship.

Everything possible needs to be done to avoid interruption and confusion in worship. Ushers may prevent the intrusion of secretaries or outsiders; announcements can be eliminated from the formal service.

Usually, this formal service should come at the close of the teaching sessions, serving as a climax to the program. This timing prevents the interruptions of late-comers. On the other hand, students arriving early can go directly to their classes and begin work at once. A work period is arranged at the opening of most elementary class sessions in good schools.

Services for children above the kindergarten and for adolescents should be definitely limited in time, between fifteen and twenty minutes long. This brevity leads to better concentration and more genuine participation.

Most worship services for children will be more effective when conducted in separate grade or age-level groups of fifteen or more children. In this way the service can be planned in terms of the group's interests and capacities. It would be an advantage in most churches, for instance, if first-grade children could learn to worship in their own group and older children would not have over two grades together except for very special events.

CONCEPTS OF GOD

The concepts of God should be Christian and worthy. Some of the following will be suggestive:

God is an eternal God who was never created. He is from everlasting to everlasting.

God is dependable and works in dependable ways. He does not lose his temper and send a flood or a tornado. He "sends rain on the just and the unjust alike."

God creates the order which sustains the universe.

God sustains and undergirds his creation; otherwise it would not exist.

God is love.

God's whole plan for man's relationship to man is an order of love.

All people of every race and nation are loved by God. They are all his children.

God loves the bad and the good people alike.

God is always seeking each person's love and devotion because he cares about them as individuals.

Jesus shows us what God is like.

God is spirit. He is not a man.

God is at work everywhere in the universe.

All people need God to make their lives complete. Separation from him leads to sin.

Genuine worship is that continuous relationship with God where he is loved and adored.

THE MERIT OF THE MATERIALS

Materials chosen for the service should be of good literary and musical quality as well as appropriate for a religious service.

The poetry should be simple in form and uncomplicated in

thought, and yet should have a beautiful sustained rhythm and real dignity of content. There are many poems of marked literary quality which children can appreciate. For instance, *The Golden Flute* (New York: John Day Co., 1932), compiled by Alice Hubbard and Adeline Babbitt, has proved of great value.

"Stopping by Woods on a Snowy Evening," by Robert Frost, can quiet our spirits to wonder. "Velvet Shoes," by Elinor Wylie, can hush our feelings in the silence of the snow. Thoughts can be turned to the needs of animals in "The Young Calves," by Robert P. Tristram Coffin. Gratitude for the seasons and God's orderly plan may be heightened by Margaret Widdemer's "Procession." "Stars," by Sara Teasdale, a lovely poem, will make us feel truly "honored to be witness of so much majesty." The security of a home is appreciated after hearing "Song for a Little House," by Christopher Morley. "Miracles," by Walt Whitman, may widen the vision of adolescents. "Stars Tonight," by Sara Teasdale (New York: The Macmillan Co., 1930), is priceless. Great poetry may lead to appreciation of the varied aspects of the universe, of homes, and of justice for many kinds of people.

Other poems include "Today," Angela Morgan; "Youth Builds," Mary Carolyn Davies; "America First," George Aston Oldham; "Glory to Them," Anderson M. Scruggs; "My Religion," Leo Tolstoi; "Beauty," Nancy Byrd Turner; "The Great Wide World," William Brighty Rands; "I Took a Day to Search for God," Bliss Carman; "Trees," Joyce Kilmer; and "Alone in the Night," Sara Teasdale.

If stories are told, they need to be carefully prepared and arranged. Leaders will do well to study *The Storyteller in Religious Education,* by Jeanette Perkins Brown (Boston: Pilgrim Press, 1951) and *Bequest of Wings,* by Annis Duff (New York: The Viking Press, 1944) or *The Proof of the Pudding,* by Phyllis Fenner (New York: John Day Co., 1957). Many good stories from children's books can be cut, condensed, and rearranged. In the chapter on themes will be found books containing useful material for elementary ages as well as for young people.

At Christmas time Eric Kelly's *The Christmas Nightingale* (New York: Macmillan Co., 1946) will provide some Polish stories. Ruth Sawyer's *The Long Christmas* (New York: Viking Press, 1941) and Alice Dalgliesh's *Christmas* (New York: Charles Scribner's Sons, 1950) provide several kinds of resources. Ruth Sawyer's *The Christmas Anna Angel* (New York: Macmillan Co., 1950) will captivate the listener who hears about this Hungarian child. If one is fortunate enough to have *The Man Who Gave Us Christmas* by Winifred M. Kirkland (New York: Woman's Press, 1940) they will surely use this story of Luke with older groups in the Christmas season.

For other occasions there are *The Christmas Story Caravan* by Anna P. Broomell (Philadelphia: J. B. Lippincott Co.), and *Greatness Passing By* by Hulda Niebuhr (New York: Charles Scribner's Sons, 1931). Kate Seredy's *Tree for Peter* (New York: Viking Press, 1941) is a moving story of a little boy who grew up in Shanty Town and while young set about to rebuild it into a place of beauty. Also recommended is Ruth W. Russell's *Stories You Can Tell* (Valley Forge: Judson Press, 1963).

In other chapters, we have dealt with the importance of good music and poetry in the hymns and songs used for worship and with prayers and litanies.

Among the basic considerations in creating worship experiences is the art of sensing the capacities and understandings of the different ages. All materials used should be selected with the students' needs in mind. They are to respond and to worship in the here and now, not in some future condition. The content of the service must touch and give meaning to their own life situations. They need to be helped to relate varied aspects of their life in their present condition.

Children and youth are people, truly as much as are adults, with their own interests, questions, problems, feelings, and psychological development.

The tendency in much prepared worship material is to keep it too abstract, general, and symbolic, while children tend to think concretely and are not much affected by the general and the abstract. They need resources which speak to them at their age and where they live now. Perspective changes for young folks from year to year. They see life and its meanings from new angles as they add years and experiences to their lives.

Leaders must ask whether a particular group of children are ready psychologically to enter into the materials and content of the service. If a service is relevant to the Thanksgiving season for younger children, it cannot be laden with abstract and figurative statements about "the bounty of the harvest" or "the beauty of the autumnal earth" or "for the food we eat."

Instead, these must be translated into vivid, dramatic, authentic processes and conditions. Actual stories of some of the thousands of people involved in feeding us can portray something of our interdependence and of our great debt to such people. Scientific processes in the improvement of agriculture and the preservation of goods may portray some of the miracles of God's order which man is discovering and using.

Formal Worship for Older Children and Young People

In a short, formal service of worship for older children and young people, there seem to be three major steps involved:

1. The unification and common focus of the congregation. A processional hymn, a call to worship, a response or doxology, and a hymn may serve to unite the people.

2. An imaginative presentation of some life situation to be revalued and to bring concreteness to the service. This may

involve the motivation of an offering and its presentation, and a talk or a story.

3. Then should follow the crystallization and formation of an attitude or a decision in some forward social purpose. This can be brought about through the careful choice of Scripture following the story or talk, the prayer silent and oral, and a hymn which emphasizes the theme and the ultimate purpose of the service, and the benediction.

SUGGESTIONS FOR A VESPER SERVICE FOR YOUNG PEOPLE

1. Possible Settings

The meeting may be held on a hilltop, or beside a lake or stream, or in some woodland spot.

It may be held in some shady spot on the church lawn, or in the yard of some member of the congregation, or in a public park.

If an outdoor service is held, it should be so timed that the middle of the meeting occurs just as the sun is setting.

If an indoor meeting is held, the room should be made very comfortable, the chairs should be in a semicircle, and everything should suggest a family group.

2. Leadership and Preparation

The committee to plan the service should be at work for at least two or three weeks before the meeting.

There may be a single leader, or different members may be assigned to take leadership at different points (one for prayers, one for poetry, etc.) without announcement.

There should be an effort to get as many as possible to participate, although the main parts should be given only to those who will prepare carefully and will make a serious effort to read or speak impressively.

Every item should be carefully prepared in advance; those who are to read should practice their parts aloud a number of times so that they are sure of themselves and can be heard.

There should be few, if any, announcements of parts. A typewritten program is often helpful.

The vesper service should not be long, between twenty and forty-five minutes.

3. Suggested Resources

Hymns: "Summer Suns Are Glowing," "This Is My Father's World," "Lord of All Being," "When Morning Gilds the Skies," "For the Beauty of the Earth," "Day Is Dying in the West," "Bring, O Morn, Thy Music," "Day Is Done" (Taps), "My God, I Thank Thee," "O Worship the King," "Joyful, Joyful, We Adore Thee."

Scripture readings (God in nature, as the Psalmists saw him): Psalms 8; 19:1-6; 29; 95:1-7; 104; 147:7-20; 148.

Meditation: In addition to silent meditation, silent prayer, and prayers and litanies written by members of the group, various young people may speak briefly on "What Causes Me to Wonder in Nature," "How I Understand God in Relation to Nature," or "The Most Helpful Experience I Have Had, in Studying Nature."

Inspirational readings:

God is to me that creative Force, behind and in the universe, who manifests Himself as energy, as life, as order, as beauty, as thought, as conscience, as love, and Who is self-revealed supremely in the creative Person of Jesus of Nazareth, and operative in all Jesus-like movements in the world to-day.

— Henry Sloane Coffin [1]

> God of the earth, the sky, the sea,
> Maker of all above, below,
> Creation lives and moves in Thee;
> Thy present life through all doth flow.
>
> *— Samuel Longfellow*

[1] *My Idea of God,* by Joseph Fort Newton (Boston: Little, Brown & Co., 1926), p. 125.

Poems should be assigned, studied, and read aloud in advance of the meeting or prepared by a group as choral reading. Usually, it is better to read the poems than to recite them, unless the participants feel quite sure that they are able to repeat them without faltering.

7.
Arrangement of a Formal Worship Service

WHEN PREPARING A FORMAL WORSHIP EXPERIENCE for or with children and young people, it is important to think of their human needs and capacities so that there will be the fewest possible distractions and limitations to their awareness of the place of God in their lives.

Order and beauty should be kept in mind so that these occasions will become memorable. In the author's Saturday School it was found that the primary- and junior-age children liked worship most of all. It was dependable and orderly in its procedure and it was beautiful and meaningful to the age for which each service was prepared. Carefully trained adults usually led these services and thus gave a Christian witness and maturity to the occasion.

Worship is not an occasion for people to stand before a group to be seen, to practice on a violin or piano, or to sing poor solos. Worship is not an occasion where individuals are to put on a show. Everything possible should be done to lead to the glorification of God, to the lifting of the mind from self-centeredness to God's ways, and to the renewal of the worshiper's mind, motives, and spirit.

There have been few books to turn to by religious educators interested in worship education. Probably the best have been those for elementary grades prepared by Jeanette Perkins Brown (see Chapter 14). However, the writer differs with her use of formal worship occasions for discussions. Such discussions should be limited to class sessions, which may of course often lead to informal worship. In a formal service, participation by the worshiper is enlisted through hymns, responses, offering, prayers, and meditation, rather than discussion.

Preparation for a formal worship service requires considerable time. Hymns, responses, processionals, offering procedures, all need ample practice in a worship training period. Between fifteen and twenty minutes should be sufficient time for the worship service itself. The theme generally requires a series of from six to eight weekly services for meaningful development. Often it may come to a climax on a special day such as Thanksgiving or Christmas, or at the close of a service enterprise or a season.

To come to the place of worship in good order and in a quiet mood is important: An orderly line of each class moving in a procession is effective. Whether in Sunday or vacation church school, it is usually well to have the formal service climax the work of the classes, the pupils having begun their class work on arrival. In a one-hour program for grades one to twelve, about 45 minutes should be allotted to class work and 15 minutes to worship or to worship training.

Rehearsal and training in worship will take the place of formal worship about two Sundays each month if schools are limited to one-hour periods. In schools with longer sessions, and in camps or vacation schools, a definite period of thirty or thirty-five minutes can be set aside to learn hymns, introits, and responses; how to take up an offering, how to walk in a processional, how to pray and to deal with questions about God, and what worship means.

In the following order of worship the author attempts to lead to a climax in prayer so that the worshiper may praise, evaluate, ask for forgiveness, express aspiration, or dedicate himself to God, depending on the service.

Provision is made for a processional as a means of entering the chapel or room when several classes of older children or young people meet together for worship. The singing brings everyone actively into the service from the very beginning and prevents disorder and conversation. Even if a single group is worshiping in its own room, rearranged for the service, it is often very helpful to have the class process to its center of worship. If this procedure is not practicable, the service may open with a call to worship by the leader, followed by a response and then an opening hymn.

The offering is received early in the service (unless it is the climax of the theme) in order that the concreteness of the theme (story or talk or drama or film) may be followed by Scripture, prayer, and a hymn which unites all of these elements in an emphasis that leads to some thoughtful decision about recognition of the rule of God.

AN ORDER OF WORSHIP

Processional

When several classes meet together for worship, it has been found helpful to go to the room for worship, singing in a processional.

(1) Plan so that the class or group assembles in good order and sings one stanza before moving. Keep pupils an arm's length apart as they move.

(2) Sing the hymn or stanza until all are in the chapel or place of worship, and then conclude with the Amen and be seated.

(3) A good processional hymn for older groups is "Joyful, Joyful, We Adore Thee"; and for primary children, "Softly, We Will Walk as to Church We Go."

(4) Usually it is well to have the two ushers lead the processional and sit in the center of the front row of seats. In most schools, the adult leader and any student participant will precede the ushers so that the children are guided throughout the service by mature leadership. Other teachers will take their places with their own groups.

The adults who lead the service will have seats at either side of the worship center. In some situations it is well to have the worship leader in his place for the service in order to help the group to feel an atmosphere of reverence and to see what to do. Leaders of worship will remove their wraps. Some leaders may wish to wear choir gowns. If there is a youth choir, its members may wear gowns or capes and lead the processional to the place of worship.

Call to Worship

(1) The call to worship may be spoken by the leader (who has risen from his position in front of the group) to remind the children that this is an occasion to think of God.

(2) This call to worship may be memorized in advance (in the worship training period) by the children and used orally for several weeks to begin the services.

(3) It should always be spoken clearly and effectively.

(4) Suggestions (see also Chapter 15):

> Surely the Lord is in this place.
>
> — *Genesis 28:16*

> From the rising of the sun to its setting
> The name of the Lord is to be praised.
>
> — *Psalm 113:3*

> The heavens are telling the glory of God;
> And the sky shows forth the work of his hands.
>
> — *Psalm 19:1* [1]

[1] *The Complete Bible: An American Translation,* J. M. Powis Smith, trans. (Chicago: The University of Chicago Press, 1939).

He makes his sun rise on the evil and on the good.
> — *Matthew 5:45b*

O give thanks to the Lord, for he is good,
For his steadfast love endures forever
> —*1 Chronicles 16:34*

Let the peoples praise thee, O God;
Let all the peoples praise thee!
> — *Psalm 67:5*

Musical Response

(1) This response is to create a further sense of the presence of God and is sung by the group.

(2) *The Sanctus, Holy, Holy, Holy,* by Alfred R. Gaul, or the chorus from "Day Is Dying in the West," or "The Earth Is Full of the Loving Kindness of the Lord" in Edith Lovell Thomas's *Sing, Children, Sing* (Nashville: Abingdon Press, 1939), may be used with all ages above kindergarten.

Offering

(1) When the leader rises and takes the offering plates from the worship center, this is the signal for the ushers to step forward and to stand before him.

(2) The leader then gives a motivating thought for the gifts such as: "We are glad to give our gift of money today because it helps us to have a warm church," or "to have lovely books and pictures in our class," or "to send Bibles to the people of Africa," or "to help to rebuild our mission school in Haiti which was destroyed by the hurricane." A new phase of the work for which the money is spent should be emphasized each week.

(3) The leader then gives the plates to the ushers while music is played and the offering is taken up.

(4) As the ushers come forward together, the audience rises.

(5) The leader takes the plates and holds them while a

suitable prayer is sung, such as "All Things Come of Thee O Lord" or "Father Bless the Gifts We Bring Thee."

Concreteness

A story or talk that develops the theme concretely is given next by the leader. The contents should center on *one concrete aspect of the topic.* For example, leading up to Thanksgiving, a series of services may be built around the struggle for religious freedom in America among the early settlers. One of these may be devoted to Roger Williams, one to William Penn, and one to the meaning of the Statue of Liberty. With such a theme this talk or story should lead to a prayer of thanksgiving or aspiration. There may well be a series of services on "Thanksgiving for People Who Help Feed Us" concentrating on one kind of worker at each service.[2]

Scripture or Poetry

(1) Following the talk or story, a brief quotation from Jesus or a mosaic of Scripture may be given by the leader or read from a poster in choral fashion by the whole group—or, better still, given from memory by the group. This same passage is used during the several weeks of one theme.[3]

(2) The Scripture or poetry should make emphatic some one viewpoint in the theme of the service. It may be chosen to evaluate or to bring to focus some central idea. The Scripture is brief enough and definite enough to create the testing of what has gone before. For example, a portion of 1 Corinthians 13:4-8 may be very effective after the concreteness in some stories or meditations. Following are some other possibilities:

> And he made from one every nation of men to live on the face of the earth.
>
> — *Acts 17:26a*

---

[2] See Chapter 5 for various examples of theme development.
[3] See Chapter 15 for further suggestions.

Have we not all one Father? Has not one God created us?
— *Malachi 2:10a*

He who loves God should love his brother also.
— *John 4:21b*

No man has ever seen God; if we love one another, then God abides in us, and his love is perfected in us.
— *1 John 4:12*

For all who are led by the spirit of God are sons of God.
— *Romans 8:14*

Prayer

(1) Silence may be used effectively after the Scripture by introducing it with one suitable suggestion related to the theme: "Let us close our eyes and think silently with God about [one idea]." This silent period may at first be only a few seconds and in time grow to a minute or more.

(2) An oral prayer is the climax toward which the whole service should move. It should gather up the thanksgiving and the aspiration worked out in the story and be carefully connected with the theme. Examine some prayers in Chapter 19. See others in the Chapter "Litanies and Responsive Readings," or the Chapter, "Lord, Teach Us to Pray." Avoid too much abstraction. Be vivid and clear. Use short sentences with children and one concrete idea at a time.

(3) Let the choir, if there is one, sing an Amen at the close of the oral prayer.

Recessional or Closing Hymn

(1) Select a hymn that emphasizes the theme.

(2) Sing one stanza before moving in a recessional.

(3) In some schools the worship group may move into a circle while singing and before concluding with the Amen.

(4) At this time notices or suggestions about the service may be given.

Benediction (Said or Sung)

A Suggested Worship Service

(For use in junior high grades at the close of a work day for Christ)

WORKING FOR CHRIST

Chapel in darkness except for candles at table and overhead light.

Call to Worship

Know that the Lord is God!
It is he that hath made us and we are his; we are his people.
For the Lord is good; his steadfast love endures forever; and his faithfulness to all generations.
Enter his gates with thanksgiving, and his courts with praise! Give thanks to him, bless his name.
Serve the Lord with gladness! come into his presence with singing!

—Psalm 100, rearranged

Sanctus

Sung *a capella* from rear of the chapel.

(Chapel lights turned on)

Hymn — "All People that on Earth Do Dwell"

Scripture

And God made from one every nation of men to live on all the face of the earth.

—Acts 17:26a

And this commandment we have from him, that who loves God should love his brother also.

—1 John 4:21

See what love the Father has given us, that we should be called children of God; and so we are.

—1 John 3:1a

Love is patient and kind; love is not jealous or boastful; it is not arrogant or rude.
Love does not insist on its own way; it is not irritable or resentful; it does not rejoice at wrong, but rejoices in the right.
Love bears all things, believes all things, hopes all things, endures all things. Love never ends.

—1 Corinthians 13:4-8a

Beloved, let us love one another; for love is of God and he who loves is born of God and knows God.

—1 John 4:7

Bringing of Gifts

Prayer

O God, we praise thee for giving us this good opportunity to come together and worship thee.

We thank thee for the Work Day for Christ, when boys and girls like us do manual labor in thy name all over our dear land, and for making us part of this group which is concerned about the welfare of others.

We thank thee for the power of young people to work together to make this world a better place to live in.

We thank thee for our parents who permitted us to come today to work and for those who gave us work to do.

Lord, we pray that the money we have earned may go to help those lacking food or drink or clothing or education, the sick, the blind, the maimed, both in our homeland and abroad.

We pray for those who are less privileged than we. Enable us to realize that they are our brothers, and help us to do our part in making their condition better.

O God, who sent us Jesus who chose to serve rather than be served, we would put back into thy care all that thou hast given us, rededicating to thy service all the powers of our mind and body, and all our worldly goods.

In the spirit of Jesus. Amen.

Hymn — "O Master Workman of the Race"

Benediction

Sanctify, O Lord, both our coming in and our going forth; and grant that when we leave thy house, we may not leave thy presence, but be thou ever near unto us and keep us near unto thee, through Jesus Christ our Lord. Amen.

8.
The Young Child
and Worship

LEARNING TO WORSHIP GOD in the early years of a child's life depends very much on the adults around him, the environment in which he lives, and his concepts of God.[1]

It is said that the baby feels love by the way he is fed and bathed and touched. When love is lacking then, the God revealed by Jesus does not reach the child. It was Bronson Alcott who declared that he had always known that God is love. No one told him, but he learned it from his mother's smile.

Genuine love has been found to have healing power in some hospitals where children are separated from their parents. An older woman, probably a grandmother, comes five days a week for six hours a day and imparts "loving care." While loving the child this woman emotionally may be able to let the child go when the time comes for his return to his family. Her powers of healing have proven remarkable.

Since the Christian message is that of a God of love seeking people to do his will and to love one another, it can best

[1] See *Man's Need and God's Action*, by Reuel L. Howe (New York: Seabury Press, 1953).

be communicated through an environment in the home, the nursery school, and the kindergarten where God's spirit is manifest in the adult's actions and motives.

As Mrs. Edith Mumford wisely says in her *Understanding Our Children* (New York: Longmans, Green & Co., 1938), "No one can create religion for another, even for a little child; all we can do is to help him discover for himself the underlying meaning of all his own experiences and to put them together. He will find God then for himself."

THE INNER SPIRIT

Rabindranath Tagore of India once wrote:

There are circumstances in which the imbibing of religion should be as easy for children as taking breath. But this very taking of breath may be put beyond the doctor's aid by the slightest obstructions. In fact, if the patient is conscious of an effort in breathing, that is a bad sign. It is the same with religion. When spiritual feeling permeates a community, then the religious life is spontaneous; it naturally finds its creative activity and moral expression. The problem of the religious education of children does not then separately arise, because their sub-conscious mind grows in an atmosphere rich with the sense of divine presence.

Horace Bushnell said that leaders should "bathe the child in their own feeling of love of God and dependency on him . . . to make what is good, happy and attractive." [2]

Christian fellowship is rooted in God and not artificially manufactured. The Christian is called to a life centered in God as revealed by Jesus. As God has loved us, so we must love. In a genuine sense, this love is not a law, but the essence of our relationship to God.

We need to think more of the inner feelings and ideas of the child and much less of outward practices, forms, and creeds; we need to plan his religious education in relation to

[2] *Discourses on Christian Nurture,* by Horace Bushnell (Boston: Massachusetts Sabbath School Society, 1847), p. 56.

these inner conditions. He needs help in understanding relationships among peoples and the mysteries of life and death. A valuable book dealing with the religious growth of the child from one to seven is *Your Growing Child and Religion,* by the English chaplain, R. S. Lee (New York: The Macmillan Co., 1963).

The parents and other adult leaders should receive from the church far more education and guidance in their own faith and worship than many of them do at present, so that they may be prepared to live as Christians with children.

PRAYING

When adults learn to express the need for God's forgiveness and that of others, including children, they are paving the way for genuine religion and worship.

Praying at bedtime with very young children may be done largely by the adults. Its value will depend upon the sincerity of the worshiper and the connection of the prayer with the particular and immediate experiences of the child and the people involved. Prayers about abstractions become meaningless and monotonous. The vocabulary should be within range of the child's understanding.

Saying prayers may not be the same as praying. Praying involves the mind and the will. It is not ceremony and form. It should be a part of the process of growing to love God with the heart, the mind, and all of one's powers.

One day a mother was seated at the window with her two young children. They were enjoying the beauty of the sunset on a lovely landscape covered with snow. In the course of their happy conversation, one of the children said, "If I could, I would fly out to God and give him a big hug."

Here the relationship between God and his beautiful creation had started, and here was worship.

While closing the day with Mark, their five-year-old son, the father read *God Planned It That Way,* by Carolyn Muller

(Nashville: Abingdon Press, 1952). Then the two of them together sang, three times, "God We Love You Best of All." Spontaneously, Mark then prayed to God: "We love you because you work so hard planning everything. You even plan trees. That's hard work to plan a tree with all those things on it. You work so hard you need everybody in the whole world to help you. We are sorry when we don't. Help us to do the things we should. Thank you, God."

Conversations leading to praying at home or with individuals or small groups may grow out of the lovely picture book, *A Child's Grace* by Constance Bannister, ed. (New York: E. P. Dutton & Co., 1938).

A few memorized prayers for kindergarten children may be suggestive in learning to pray. Some may be found in *My Prayer Book*, by Margaret Clemens (Chicago: Rand McNally & Co., 1947) and *First Prayers for Little Children*, by Mary Alice Jones, ed. (Chicago: Rand McNally & Co., 1942).

Such a prayer as follows may be said or sung in the morning:

> Father, we thank thee for the night,
> And for the pleasant morning light,
> For health and food and loving care,
> And all that makes the day so fair.
> Help us to do the things we should,
> To be to others kind and good;
> In all we do, in work or play,
> To grow more loving every day. Amen.[3]

NURSERY CHILDREN AND WORSHIP

Nursery children are not usually ready for group worship experiences. Their best occasion, however, for prayer in a school is when they gather at a table for a drink of fruit

[3] By Rebecca J. Weston. From *Songs and Games for Little Ones*, by Gertrude Walker and Harriet S. Jenks (Boston: Oliver Ditson Company). Used by permission of Theodore Presser Company.

juice or tomato juice; at home, there is opportunity at bedtime or at the family table.

Of course, moments of worship should be recognized in the midst of all kinds of experiences. Such occasions can be very meaningful. For example —

"Listen to the birds," said the teacher as six nursery school children were leisurely emerging from the woods one bright, sunny day in early spring.

"What does it mean, Miss Brookmead?" asked three-and-a-half-year-old John.

"I don't know what they are saying," answered the teacher. "I guess they are glad for this springtime. I am glad for it too. We have had so much fun in the woods this morning. I have seen many things for which I would like to thank God: there is the pretty blue sky, the little white flowers, the water in the brook, and the trees with the little buds and leaves on them. What would you like to thank him for today?"

"For Rob's mother for making the orange juice," said Walter.

"Yes, we are thankful for her, and we will be glad to have the orange juice this morning, won't we? Is there anything else?"

"Thank him for the lovely day," said three-year-old Donald.

"All right," replied the teacher. "At the table when we have our orange juice we will thank him for many things. Would you like to make the prayer, Donald?"

"Yes, I will thank him," answered Donald.

So the group started back to the school. They went through the routine of taking off their outdoor play suits and attending to their toilet, and finally were ready for orange juice. After the napkins had been put in place the teacher said, "Donald, you said you would say our 'Thank you' to God today. Do you remember what you want to say?"

"I want to say 'Thank you for the lovely day this morning.' "

"That is right. Let us all bow our heads as Donald prays."
So Donald prayed, "Thank you God for the lovely morning." He did not say "Amen" so the teacher supplied it.

The next morning the children took another walk, this time to see some flowers in a nearby professor's yard. At the orange juice time the teacher said, "There are so many things I would like to thank God for this morning. What would you like to thank him for today?"

Again Donald said, "I want to thank him for the lovely day." So the teacher said, "That will say it all, won't it?"

Poems, songs, prayers, and conversations may contribute much to worship if the experiences can be provided. Growing plants or flowers, collecting insects like the spider or daddy-long-legs, observing snails and worms, and caring for a hamster, a mouse, a guinea pig, a goldfish, a turtle, a mother cat and her kittens, a rabbit, some baby chicks, or a farm animal — all may lead the child to the mystery of life, death, and God as Creator. To sense how God cares for his creation and his order, as well as his dependence on people, is important in worship. Out of endless experiences children may learn of God's plans for life and creation, that he is dependable and that people have a part in caring for his creatures.

Books, as well as trips, gardens, and other experiences, can add much to the child's outreach towards God. Here are a few:

Jones, Elizabeth B., *Round About Me.* Anderson, Indiana: Warner Press, 1953.

McCloskey, Robert, *Make Way for Ducklings.* New York: Viking Press, 1941.

Schultz, Florence B., *Summer with Nursery Children.* Philadelphia: United Church, 1958.

Tensen, Ruth M., *Come to the Farm.* Chicago: Reilly & Lee Co., 1949.

KINDERGARTEN CHILDREN AT WORSHIP

Kindergarten children gradually learn to gather around a teacher and be seated in a "huddle," perhaps on a rug on the floor, or in several small groups with assistant teachers. This kind of group meeting should generally come at the close of the morning in order to gather up ideas, events, and questions for the thinking of these children. Here a suitable story related to the activities of the morning, or one from a series such as *The Family Finds Out*, by Edith F. Hunter (Boston: Beacon Press, 1952), may be told. After some conversation about the story, it would be an appropriate time for the prayer. This should be vivid, concrete, and simple, perhaps eight or ten short sentences in length. Its effectiveness will depend upon its relevance to each child's experience during the immediate morning. Generally its tone will be one of praise and thanksgiving to God.

A Roman Catholic nun reported that her best approach to prayer with younger children was in connection with actual experiences. Standing beside some beautiful flowers and admiring them, she exclaimed, "Praise be to God!" One day a child drew near as she looked at some flowers and said, "I know what you are saying."

"What is it, John?" the sister asked.

"Praise be to God!" he replied.

After many years of experience guiding leaders of children, the author finds that the beginnings of recognition of God come first through sensing the adults' attitudes and practices and then through the use of experiences which have been vivid and meaningful to the child.

As already stated, worship may conclude the morning's work in the kindergarten. While children are gathering into a group (or into two or three groups) with a teacher or assisting teachers, they may talk over the morning's experiences, make some new plans, listen to an appropriate story, or recall ideas, feelings, and questions growing out of some experiences. These lead to the time for meaningful prayer. Any one of the following events will provide ideas for expressing thanksgiving and praise:

A snowstorm and the fun of playing in the snow
Preparing a birds' Christmas tree and placing food on it
A trip to a farm to see young animals and the processes of God's world of growing things
Seeing a moth emerge
Seeing some baby chickens or kittens
Making cookies for an aged friend
Planting seeds in a box or a garden
Seeing a baby and learning about its care
A trip to a garden
Happy rhythms
Dramatic play in a home-making corner
Building furniture
Looking at a favorite book, like *Let's Go Outdoors,* by Harriet E. Huntington (Garden City: Doubleday & Co., 1939)

It takes some years before young children develop any accurate feeling and understanding of God. They may witness adults at worship and sense that there is a Power beyond what they can see. Many experiences should be fostered that lead to such an awareness. Creating an awareness of mystery in living things can be a helpful step. The marvel of little chickens coming out of a shell, or life developing in the form of leaves and flowers from a bulb or from seeds which children plant, or a butterfly creeping out of a cocoon—such things are types of experiences which, with variations, adults can foster reverently, again and again.

The rapt responses of children, their questions and comments, often reflect a slowly developing sense of the mystery of life and the world which they can see. The singing of songs related to these experiences, the encouragement of children's own reactions may be stages in cultivating sensitivity to the Eternal at orange-juice time or in the kindergarten group meeting. At the close of the session, children may think over their experiences and a capable teacher may express their wonder and appreciation in a prayer like this:

> O God, on this cold bright sunny day, we thank you for this pleasant warm church. We thank you for our warm comfortable snow suits and mittens. We are happy that we have such warm clothes to wear. We are glad that the sun is shining to help warm the air. We thank you for our kindergarten and our friends here. It is fun to build a house and to think of the many nice things that we have in our homes. It is fun to play with sister and to help mother wash the dishes and to help daddy shovel the snow. We thank you, dear God, for our homes. Amen.

THE FIRST GRADE

Insofar as possible, six-year-old children should have most of their worship experiences with their own age. On some occasions they may join their parents in the sanctuary for a half-hour family service. At special times they may join another primary grade. They will grow and learn more, however, if worship usually comes as a part of their own group experience and is related to their own concrete events.

At the beginning of the term, time should be set aside for talking about and learning simple hymns such as may be found in Edith Lovell Thomas' *Sing, Children, Sing* (*op. cit.*). The religious ideas in these may be connected with a picture, a trip, or other concrete data.

Bringing money for a specific near-at-hand, well-understood objective can be a part of worship if adequately motivated by a prepared leader.

The group meeting, after the work period of a class, will include planning, reporting on their work, a story or a film, and conversation. This may end with a prayer and a hymn. More formal worship may come toward the close of the year as preparation for the second grade.

Imagine a first-grade class seated in a semicircle around their teacher and facing a wall with the Elsa Anna Wood picture "The Lord of Joy" on it. Under it on a low table could be a small Christmas tree.

The children have talked about their school and the number of weeks before Christmas. Then the teacher leads them in singing Christmas songs from *Martin and Judy Songs* by Edith Lovell Thomas (Boston: Beacon Press, 1959). The children are reminded that Christmas is Jesus' birthday. Here is the spontaneous conversation that developed with one group:

STEVE: Christmas is Jesus' birthday.

JOAN: Jesus is God because when God was a little boy his name was Jesus [note confusion].

ANTHONY: He was not a little boy, just a spirit.

TEACHER: What do you mean by spirit?

FRED: I think when people die they are spirits and then go up to God.

STEVE: God is right here now [pointing to the group].

PAM: He is here [pointing to her heart].

STEVE: We can walk through him because he is a spirit.

JOAN: We can't see God.

PAM: He is a man, but you can't see him, but he is right here.

ANTHONY: I think he flies because we can't see him.

JOAN: When we die we fly up to God.

FRED: They bury you six feet down in the ground when you die.

MARY: I think God was a man but he died.

JOAN: If someone hurt God and he died, he would still be alive the next day.

STEVE: His spirit would still be alive.

ANTHONY: It would die.

The children then went on to talk about the death of their pets and other animals they had seen.

Here were problems for the teacher that would need many weeks of discussion. At the close of such conversations might come the right moment for a suitable prayer by the teacher and perhaps a simple hymn.

Books like the following contain useful stories for these first-grade conversations:

Jones, Mary Alice, *Tell Me About God* (*op. cit.*).
Manwell, Elizabeth, *Always Growing* (*op. cit.*).

Muller, Carolyn, *God Gave Us Seasons*. Nashville: Abingdon Press, 1958.

Watson, Jane Werner, *My Golden Book About God*. New York: Golden Press, 1957.

Wensberg, Katherine, and Mary Northrop, *The Tuckers*. Boston: Beacon Press, 1952.

Here are materials near to the lives of these children and where suitable understanding of God may grow.

OLDER PRIMARIES

More regular prayer in the home, worship training sessions to learn hymns and responses for worship, opportunities to learn about giving and to think about worship and experience formal worship services are all important parts of the special period which is provided in each session for education in worship.

Themes for worship, the order of worship, and music are discussed in Chapters 5, 7 and 13.

Learning to pray should be a part of the program in second and third grades. Such books as follow will be useful:

Bro, Margueritte H., *More Than We Are* (*op. cit*) (for the thinking of parents and teachers).

Jones, Mary Alice, *My Own Book of Prayers*. New York: Rand McNally, 1938.

————, *Tell Me About Prayer* (*op. cit.*).

McGavran, Grace W., *And When You Pray*. Boston: Pilgrim Press, 1941.

Booklets for worship in the home need to be discussed with parents, and guidance given them in prayer.

For the children, *Thoughts of God,* published until March 1962, four times a year by the Connecticut Council of Churches, has been the classic worship resource that has served families all around the world for many years. Some of its best materials have been collected in two volumes previously cited: *Thoughts of God for Boys and Girls,* by Welker and Barber, and *As We Think with God,* by Maramarco and Welker.

Stories for use in the formal worship service will be found in Chapter 16. The following books on primary worship and resources are most valuable:

Brown, Jeanette P., *As Children Worship.* Boston: Pilgrim Press, 1936.
————, *Children's Worship in the Church School.* New York: Harper & Row, 1939.
————, *More Children's Worship in the Church School.* New York: Harper & Row, 1953.

Some collections of stories are:

Jones, Mary Alice, *Tell Me About Heaven.* Chicago: Rand McNally & Co., 1956.
Kunhardt, Dorothy, *Once There Was a Little Boy.* New York: Viking Press, 1946.
————, *God-Creator* (second grade reader). Greenwich: Seabury Press, 1964.
Stevens, Bertha, *How Miracles Abound* (story pamphlets) (*op. cit.*).

As children come in wider contact with life, they must face all kinds of problems of suffering, disaster, injury, and death. The Christian cannot say that all of these happenings are the will of God, even though God's will is involved in all of life. If evil, tragic, and unpleasant things happen in a child's world, they must be faced. Some of these experiences must be involved in the worship of God.

Perhaps a few principles may be helpful to the leader, the parent, and the teacher of children. In all kinds of situations, God is always loving his children. Never can we say to a child, "God will not love you, if . . ." God is seeking the good in and for his children. He can help us, when we are in trouble, to face life courageously and in love. When we do wrong, he is seeking us.

It is important to recognize the chain of events in an orderly world that may cause many ills, when men are selfish, noncooperative, careless, ignorant, unloving, prejudiced, indifferent to God's will and order in the world. Here are endless realms in which people need to learn to work with God and to show his love. People must be co-workers with God.

Stories of the constructive ways in which many kinds of people work with God's order to help people and to make life good need to be found and told. These persons need not be famous to deserve this use for worship.

There are situations like earthquakes, floods, and storms which cause great disaster. Why we have these may not be fully understood. Doubtless research will enable men to do much more about these matters. Again man in his freedom has responsibility. Children need this challenge to become discoverers in order that they may *serve* people and realize God's will.

Religion is not an escape from life or its problems. Devotion to the will of God should lead one to meet life triumphantly and in love.

One day when some primary children were saddened by the account of some homeless children, they asked, "Why doesn't God help them?" Instead of praying to God to assume this responsibility, the leader began first to guide the children in thinking about their own part. She showed them how men and women needed to work on these conditions. She told about a man who was spending his life in trying to find homes for just such children and how money was needed for his work. Out of this grew a plan among the children to help this man in his work with money. This gift of money was a source of much love and joy.

Now a prayer expressing gratitude for this man and others who were helping homeless children could be offered. The prayer included an expression of their own love and an awareness of God's desire for people's help and love.

9.
Facing Problems
in Learning to Pray

ALL CHRISTIANS WOULD PROBABLY AGREE that they ought to pray. Yet (if one may judge from the comments of leaders, parents, and young people) it seems evident that many are puzzled and fearful and have little confidence in their own ability to pray. As they become more frank in this admission they often say, "No one has ever taught us how to pray," or "We do not know what it is all about."

Grou, an older writer, says that we come to God in prayer in calamity. Then we turn away when the emergency has passed. Necessities and accidents of life are the main matter and motive of the prayers of the majority of Christians.[1]

SOME OF THE PROBLEMS

Experience in teaching young people frequently reveals that they are confused when trying to pray. Out of this confusion has come skepticism and the abandonment of prayer. For example, here are some of the confused ideas some children and youth may hold:

[1] *How to Pray,* by Jean-Nicolas Grou, tr. by Joseph Dalby, D.D. (New York: Harper & Row, 1956).

(1) God is often considered to be a Santa Claus to give people things they want: "I asked God to help me be good — but I was disgusted the next day when I was punished, and I blame God for it."

(2) Prayer is often asking for favors — never praising or thanking God or feeling a fellowship with him or seeking his will.

(3) God is thought of as located on a high throne, with people at his feet begging for favors.

(4) There is confusion about God's hearing people everywhere at the same time.

(5) God seems only to listen to prayers at night.

(6) Prayer is regarded only as words memorized in a certain form.

(7) Asking God to punish people is thought of as a form of prayer.

(8) God's failure to prevent a child from getting into trouble may be considered a failure of prayer.

(9) Some who pray expect God to change the laws of the universe for their particular wishes. Mark Twain's *Huckleberry Finn* reminds us of much of the confusion about the usual idea of prayer as petition.

> Miss Watson she took me in the closet and prayed, but nothing come of it. She told me to pray every day, and whatever I asked for I would get it. But it warn't so. I tried it. Once I got a fishline, but no hooks. It warn't any good to me without hooks. I tried for the hooks three or four times, but somehow I couldn't make it work. By and by, one day, I asked Miss Watson to try for me, but she said I was a fool. She never told me why, and I couldn't make it out no way. I set down one time back in the woods, and had a long think about it. I says to myself, if a body can get anything they pray for, why don't Deacon Winn get back the money he lost on pork? Why can't the widow get back her silver snuffbox that was stole? Why can't Miss Watson fat up? No, says I to myself, there ain't nothing in it.[2]

2 (New York: Harper & Row, 1904), p. 28.

(10) Too many people do not allow God to guide them in their praying. A child's idea of God is a basic factor in the development of his prayer life. During his early years, the child begins to ask questions about God. Where is he? Can I see him? Can he see me? It is during these years that he forms his ideas of God, influenced perhaps by phrases from adult comments, from hymns, stories, prayers, and conversations. God may be thought of as a magician who will give him whatever he asks for — provided he asks in the right way, or God may be someone who spies upon him and will punish him if he does wrong, or one who will change conditions to protect him. Sentimental, weird, magical, anthropomorphic, and untrue concepts of God hamper the prayer life.

Adults who teach about prayer may need to keep before themselves some of the important Christian ideas of God:

(1) God is always present and never waits for man to bring him near. Even when we ignore him, forget him, or rebel against him, God is actively seeking us. When we pray, God is reaching out to us and seeking our fellowship.

(2) God is different from man. He is creator, while man is creature. God is completely independent of every other creature. Man is dependent on God as the "Ground of all Being." God is the Eternal. Man is becoming, but God "was in the beginning, is now, and ever shall be, world without end."

(3) God is the origin and source of everything that has existence. Creatures exist only in such a form and over such a life span as is within the framework of God's will, but God himself is the creative, preserving action that keeps our universe from nothingness. God is the *cause*.

(4) God's love for man is constant. It is uncaused love. No one merits it or earns it, but all need it and should accept it. "God is love."

(5) God will teach us how to pray if we love him and accept him. Properly to pray means that the heart or inner

voice listens and expresses love for God. The germ of love is the source of real prayer. Prayer is more than words. God understands our feelings and inner desires and attitudes. This insight is basic in genuine prayer. The worshiper's heart should be full of conscious aspirations toward God, for God seeks these. We begin to pray by adoring God and what he wills and represents in all of life.

(6) "God is spirit," and cannot be formed into an image such as an old man on a cloud, nor any figure in any one place. God is dependable. He cannot be changed by man's pleadings. His love is constant but uncaused. He is "the same today, yesterday, and forever."

A set time, place, or manner for prayer may lead the child to believe that God can be sought only in this way. Such an idea is not so unlike the pagan notion of attracting the attention of the gods by prostrating oneself upon the floor or by ringing bells at a certain time to awaken a sleeping god. Children will need to have varied kinds of experiences with prayer — at table, at bedtime, in the church, out of doors, and wherever they have had significant and vivid experiences of awe and wonder. Camps, vacation schools, and trips, as well as class and home occasions, may foster an awareness of God in all of life.

Continuous Growth in Prayer

A state leader working with older people has reported that many adults are in terror of death and unprepared for it. Here again is evidence of grievous neglect in Christian education, for wholesome and vital prayer would have involved a growing love and friendship with God and a Christian concept of him and his realm. Genuine preparation for later years should develop continuously from childhood.

Limitations in Prayer

About 1776, Grou wrote about how we limit ourselves in his book, *How to Pray:*

We know by heart a few forms of prayer; we find others to choose from in books; there we stop, and when we have read these or recited them by heart we imagine nothing else is required. How grievously we deceive ourselves! With all these forms, however beautiful the sentiments expressed, we do not know how to pray and mostly we do not pray; or perhaps we are praying in our own way, but we are not praying in God's way. . . . the truth is in fact that it is only spiritual souls quickened by grace who rightly pray according to God's will.[3]

Perhaps it is wise, when learning to pray, to study the prayers of others and to learn much about God as Christians. Growth in praying, however, requires much more thinking, planning, and discipline on the part of individuals. Such experiences are possible when there is sufficient guidance and adequate opportunity for study and growth in home and church.

Good materials to help parents and leaders have been scarce. It is difficult, if not impossible, to find curriculum material offering adequate help in prayer, and competent religious educators have had to draw on their own personal resources in providing such training.

It is time that the modern church began to deal with prayer in terms suited to the present day, providing the best insights of the church in this realm of Christian living, and making suitable adaptations for each age level. Prayer needs to become an integral part of worship courses, courses dealing with God, and with science and religion. When segregated from other realms of life, it may lack the incentive for practice and growth. The end product of such separation is meaninglessness. But prayer, wisely and devotedly taught, can be vital.

[3] *Op. cit.,* p. 16. Used by permission.

10.
What Is Prayer?

PERHAPS THERE IS NOTHING SO MUCH NEEDED in our time as a vital, intelligent understanding and practice of prayer. Without it Christians will lack the spiritual resources by which they shall find the power to live adequately in these changing times. It was William James who once declared that it is as important to develop the power of silence as the power of words. Prayer may become an inner communion with God.

Prayer is centered in God who loves and cares for his children. Genuine prayer involves the individual's praise, his confession, his aspiration, and his own dedication. In a sense each person is responsible for his own prayers. Praying is more than listening to the minister pray, more than reciting some memorized prayers; it is an outreach of the person to God, with the full recognition that God's will must be done. Prayer involves a fundamental honesty which exposes the self to the promptings of God. It can clarify motives and sublimate them. It is thinking with God. It is honoring God with our motives. At its highest level prayer is communion with God. Motives, attitudes, and feelings are involved. It is the inner voice where God is speaking. It is often silence without words at all. Love and adoration of God are central in prayer.

JESUS AT PRAYER

Jesus stressed that "in praying" we should "not heap up empty phrases as the Gentiles do; for they think," he said "that they will be heard for their many words" (Matthew 6:7). Nowhere does Jesus "beseech" God as in primitive religion. He prayed as if he believed that "your Father knows what you need before you ask him" (Matthew 6:8). Prayer seems to have been a condition for him of receiving power from God. He accepted God as perfect in goodness: "No one is good but God alone" (Mark 10:18). Jesus' dominant purpose was to know and to do the will of him who sent him, of God. John writes of Jesus, "I do as the Father has commanded me" (John 14:31). Jesus committed his entire self to God. Even in his time of greatest agony he said, "Not as I will, but as thou wilt" (Matthew 26:39). God's purposes are always active and they were dominant in Jesus' life. The good which Jesus did was radiant with the spirit of God.

PRAYER AS SPIRITUAL

"God is spirit." Prayer is a spiritual act. We are related to God "in spirit and in truth." It is the heart that prays. Jeremiah wrote: "You will seek me, and find me; when you seek me with all your heart" (Jeremiah 29:13). Man is reconditioned by his response to God — the response of his entire self. It involves seeking God's rule, God's kingdom. Prayer is man's closest relationship to God in life.

OFFERING OUR MOTIVES TO GOD

In the Westminster Shorter Catechism we have a concise form of the meaning of self-giving: "Prayer is the offering up of our desire unto God for things agreeable to his will." It is the heart which must act, rather than any recital of words.

It is not the honoring of God with our lips but with our motives and purposes. "Whatever you do, in work or deed, do everything in the name of the Lord Jesus, giving thanks to God the Father through him" (Colossians 3:17). This loving surrender to God brings to us a new freedom in meeting life's demands.

More than 250 years ago Nicholas Herman, better known as Brother Lawrence, lived his life for over forty years almost continuously in the presence of God. As he walked in the countryside, he began to see the providence and power of God, the transforming effects of his creation. He saw that every action, even unpleasant work, should all be done in companionship with God, holding "loving converse, without set rule or stated method," in all conditions. Prayer did not involve an altar, a sanctuary, to be authentic. It was a relationship to God in every action. He accepted the nearness of God and knew that his own life and spirit could be open to God anywhere. It is for us neither to forget God's presence nor to ignore his realty. Brother Lawrence demonstrated the way of forgetfulness of self by having his mind oriented towards God's will and purpose and so he acted for the love of God.

Since God is the source of our universe and of all goodness, genuine prayer involves recognizing him and his will in all realms of life with praise and thanksgiving. Through this relationship comes a genuine and continuing love of God. The heart of the Christian religion is the love of God, as well as its corollary, the love of all his people.

Love should lead to dedication to God's will along with one's fellows, for common action. Prestige, power, rivalry should diminish with genuine communication with God, because fundamental honesty in the presence of God who knows us better than we ourselves should lead to a true facing of our motives. Prayer should cleanse our motives, and bring them into greater harmony with God's purposes.

Adoration

Prayer begins in the recognition of God and his meaning to the worshiper. Praise, thanksgiving and adoration are basic for the one who prays. Probably prayers of praise and thanks are the ones most suited to children. Such expressions to God will lead them to awareness of the world beyond themselves and of God.

Older groups may well give expression to adoration. This more mature way of praying can come to anyone who learns to love God and grows to recognize his glory and greatness.

It has been found helpful to have in one's memory some noble expressions of adoration for use on varied occasions, particularly for private worship. A few follow:

Great is the Lord, and greatly be praised.
— *Psalm 145:3*

Thine, O Lord, is the greatness, and the power, and the glory, and the victory and the majesty; for all that is in the heavens and in the earth is thine; thine is the kingdom, O Lord, and thou art exalted as head above all.
— *1 Chronicles 29:11*

Bless the Lord, O my soul; and all that is within me, bless his holy name!
— *Psalm 103:1*

Prayer is self-giving. The gift of self is our best offering; even when we give material things, we need also to "give ourselves with our gifts."

At the start of the day we may say:

> O God, I give thee myself this day;
> To hallow thy name,
> For the coming of thy kingdom,
> To do thy will.
> Take me from myself and use me
> As thou wilt,
> Where thou wilt,
> When thou wilt,
> With whom thou wilt.

INITIATIVE OF GOD

God is always at work, creating and sustaining his universe, its order, and his love. He is always seeking his people, even when they ignore him, forget him, or rebel against him. God's love is always reaching out and responding to us. So, when we really pray with our hearts and minds, he is reaching us in fellowship. Prayer is the appropriating of this divine spirit and power which all men need. We must be continually aware that God is creator and man is creature, and so this relationship needs to be maintained continuously. We are made for fellowship with God.

Lofty prayer *is not* for the purpose of enlightening God or instructing him about the best ways by which to operate the world. On the other hand, prayer *is* communication, and an intimate relationship with God and a recognition of his concern about every one of his children and his creation.

Perhaps the words of Isaiah may serve as a corrective to the tendency to use prayer to direct God:

> Who has directed the Spirit of the Lord,
>   or as his counselor has instructed him?
> Whom did he consult for his enlightenment,
>   and who taught him the path of justice,
> and taught him knowledge,
>   and showed him the way of understanding?
>   — *Isaiah 40:13-14*

MORE THAN MAN

"No man can live to himself alone." Everything in the universe is interrelated; even our own bodies must be treated as wholes and interrelated. Though each person has boundaries and limitations, he is special and unique. At the same time he must recognize his relationship to many other people, to God's laws of the universe, and to God's pervading will and purpose. Here is a mysterious universe that contains everlasting and eternal resources. Dr. Tillich has written that "in every expression of genuine love, there is God." This is "more than we are" because it is of God.

John Donne of London declared long ago:

> The Lord is good to
> them, who on him rely,
> and to the soul that
> seeks him earnestly.

When man links up his will and motive with God, he also has mysterious powers. In the face of trial and suffering, man often rises out of himself into a new being. A new dimension is added to his life. When Jesus was on the cross, he was able to pray "Father, forgive them; for they know not what they do" (Luke 23:34).

The self-centered and selfish person tends to try to ignore this interrelationship involved in living. Naturally, such a state leads to suffering, illness, and a great limitation in the individual's development and understanding of life. Self-love and self-centered concerns may interfere with prayer.

Genuine prayer at its highest should lead supremely to the seeking and the power to do God's good, and to the acceptance of God's love in every realm of life. It is the extension of the person beyond the self-centered, so that the power of the Eternal may possess his spirit and his insights. It involves a growing confidence in God's love of him who prays, one who cares about his life and spirit. God is like a father, according to Jesus, and never withholds his good gifts. It is doubtful, however, whether this means he will give us physical gifts. His love is constant and uncaused.

There is a partnership with God when we pray. Man is dependent for so much in the world. He must recognize this dependence and at the same time grow in creativity within the great freedom which God has intended for him. Man can plan and think and meet all kinds of conditions. He is not a slave but one created "in God's image." He has vast potential when he links his spirit with God's vast resources. Prayer is an energy, the energy of God in man.

Our prayers are limited by God's world and the order which only he has created. We cannot expect to change the stars in their courses or the seasons or the causes of disease. Man cannot expect God to change the world into a chaos to suit his whims. Man has to learn to discover how to live on the earth within God's physical and orderly conditions. Man's part is to live in the framework of God's sustaining order to create the good, and to be guided by his spirit.

Pain and death will follow certain facts and conditions. However, man can gain the strength and the power to face such conditions. Here man can become more than a conqueror. Sublimity has been noted in the lives of the sick and suffering.

MAN'S RESPONSIBILITY

There seems to be no escape from the struggle of man in attaining justice and righteousness. The prophets of the Old Testament bear dramatic testimony to the role of man at work for God's purposes. Prayer is a stern discipline in bringing renewal and creative power to man in the crosses which he may have to bear.

Prayer is not a substitute for work, responsibility, devotion, and concern for God's will. To honor God involves courageous effort, concern, and realization that we are co-workers with God.

Prayer involves love of God and that, in turn, means love of his will and his purposes. It is not self-seeking but the extension of the self.

As men enter the struggle for God's moral order, they must develop love of people as well as love of God. Value is placed upon all persons, young and old, all races, all classes, and all nationalities. Such love for these is active and concerned with the facts about them. We catch glimpses of this in

Trevor Huddleston's *Naught for Their Comfort* (*op. cit.*) and in Gandhi's struggle for the Indian people. To maintain genuine love demands constant renewal with God's love, the very source.

While the author was visiting with Mr. Gandhi in Wardha, India, he told her that, whenever he found his own spirit out of harmony, he stopped his undertakings and set aside time to be renewed by God's love and spirit. This capacity to live with such power and love involves the release of God's love in our own living.

Facing Our Wrongdoing

To receive the good that is of God involves the facing of one's own limitations, mistakes, and selfishness. To pray rightly involves seeking purity of heart, the love of God, the forgiving spirit, sympathy, and concern for others.

Love of God and the purification of motives should enable the worshiper to face his own mistakes, faults, and problems in one area of life after another with ever greater sincerity and lead him to seek forgiveness.

The motive is not mere appeasement or escape from the effects of wrong doing. At first a child needs to learn to admit his fault in an atmosphere of love and understanding and thus escape the sense of estrangement which sin always creates. Sin destroys relationship and fellowship. A sense of understanding, compassion, and forgiveness by one's father and mother prepares for security and the seeking of forgiveness. The Prodigal Son could come home and be received with love. Such a condition paves the way for change.

Such experiences can help growing persons to trust God, to confess wrongdoing and to seek his forgiveness. It takes time to grow to see the meaning of selfishness, of sham, and of deceit. God has given us freedom to meet life and to learn.

Prayer that leads to the love of God and confidence in his

acceptance of all who come seeking him sincerely can prepare for the seeking of forgiveness.

At the close of a day we need to gather up its events and its meanings and face all of it with God. Again we need to accept God's spirit, seeking his forgiveness, and renewing our aspirations in his spirit.

> O Lord, thou has searched me and known me.
> Thou knowest when I sit down and when I rise up;
> Thou discernest my thoughts from afar.
> Thou searchest out my path, and my lying down,
> And art acquainted with all my ways.
> Even before a word is on my tongue,
> So, O Lord, thou knowest it altogether.
>
> — *Psalm 139:1-4*

11.
"Lord, Teach Us to Pray"

THE GREAT TEACHER IN GALILEE made it his supreme purpose to help his followers find God in their everyday lives. At times they noticed that he withdrew from the multitudes and sought quiet places where he could be alone. They saw him praying "in a certain place." Soon they discovered a relationship between the spirit and achievements of their teacher and his worship. Was this the secret of his courage to depart from the traditions and teachings of the religious leaders of his day? Was this the source of his spirit of love for all classes of people and of his devotion to their needs? Certainly there was something that made his life different.

One day some of his followers came to him and said, "Lord teach us to pray." Jesus then taught them the prayer that millions of Christians have repeated, if not prayed, for many centuries and in many tongues. Doubtless, the Lord's Prayer served as an illustration of a simple form of praying. It had phrases that were familiar to the disciples and was full of meaning for them. It was taught when they were eager to learn. It reveals the spirit of praying.

There are multitudes of people today who do not know

how to pray or how to worship. At best they may know one or two prayers such as "Now I Lay Me" or the Lord's Prayer, but still they may not know much about prayer.

In studies of several high school classes, it was discovered that young people who had attended the church school for several years were unable even to repeat with accuracy the Lord's Prayer. Probably it had been memorized before it had any real meaning, and therefore was not retained. Their ideas about prayer were vague. For them it had very little meaning. How can youth be taught something about the meaning of worship for different people? How can they have satisfactory experiences of worship for themselves? There seems to be a refrain rising from many churches over the land, "Lord teach us to pray." This very meager knowledge and experience of worship seems to be a request for help.

A sensible little booklet, *And When You Pray,* by Grace W. McGavran *(op. cit.)*, was published in 1941 by the Pilgrim Press. It has been of great value to many leaders of children. Then in 1948 *Tell Me About Prayer,* by Mary Alice Jones *(op. cit.)*, was published in attractive form by Rand McNally and Company. This is useful to parents and to teachers in a class of third or fourth grade learning to pray.

THE FIFTH GRADE STUDIES THE LORD'S PRAYER

Larry and John arrived first. Since in their school the work period was at the beginning of the church school program, they set to work at once in preparation for reports on the Lord's Prayer for the class group meeting. They had a New Testament and an elementary book by Florence Taylor, *Thine Is the Glory* (Philadelphia: Westminster Press, 1949), as well as a guide sheet for their preparation.

Later on, when all the class had gathered into their group meeting, they read together from Matthew 6:9-13, and began a discussion of its meaning:

TEACHER: "Our Father—" What does this say to us?

JOHN C.: God is Lord of all. He made us all.

LARRY: God is our Ruler. He is everybody's Father.

TEACHER: All of us then belong to one big family. All of us together are brothers. "Who are in heaven —"?

LARRY (who had read *Tell Me About Heaven,* by Mary Alice Jones in the work period) : Heaven could be everywhere since God is everywhere.

MARY BETH: Heaven could be right here when we are praising God; when we are loving each other.

TEACHER: "Hallowed be thy name—"

JOHN C.: God is holy.

MELINDA: We make his name holy in our lives when we praise him.

JANE: When we love others we make him holy because this is what he wants us to do.

TEACHER: "Thy kingdom come —"

JOHN: We are praying that God will help us do what he wants us to do.

TEACHER: When we do this then we are living in God's kingdom. We let him rule our actions, our thoughts, and our conversations.

TEACHER: "Thy will be done —"

JOHN A.: We should treat each other as we want to be treated. We should think about what God wants us to do.

TEACHER: "Give us this day our daily bread."

LARRY: This does not mean only bread, but care for our physical needs.

LAURA: Yes, we need food, sleep, and clothes.

JOHN C.: We pray that we shall live better. We need to be healthy.

TEACHER: "And forgive us our debts —"

JOHN: We owe God everything we have.

LAURA: We can show God how thankful we are by using what we have wisely.

JOHN C.: When we waste things, we sin. We need to ask for forgiveness when we do wrong.

TEACHER: "As we forgive our debtors —"

MARY BETH: We have no right to ask for forgiveness from God unless we have forgiven those who wrong us.

JOHN A.: If we don't forgive right away, it becomes harder to forgive the next time somebody wrongs us.

TEACHER: "And lead us not into temptation —"

LARRY: We pray for guidance to do right.

JOHN C.: I think we need help from God so that we shall not want to do wrong.

MARY BETH: We should think before we do anything. Suppose my mother tells me not to eat the cake. So when I see the cake I should *think* first before I do anything with it. Then I will remember that mother told me not to eat it.

LAURA: Besides, if you eat it, you will have a bad conscience; probably you even will get sick.

TEACHER: "But deliver us from evil —"

MARY BETH: We pray that God will help us overcome evil.

JOHN C.: We pray that we should want to do right.

MARY BETH: This is somewhat like saying "Lead us not into temptation."

TEACHER: Yes, they are somewhat alike. If you were hit by someone, you would feel like hitting back. But you stop and think that this is not what God wants you to do. Then you are able to overcome the feeling to do wrong.

TEACHER: "For thine is the kingdom —"

LARRY: His kingdom is not a place. We can't see it. It is in us. We can feel it when we do what God wants.

MARY BETH: It is like the heaven we were talking about.

TEACHER: Yes, when we let God rule our lives then we can say we belong to God's kingdom. This kingdom which we cannot see or touch is very real in the lives of people because it belongs to the rule of God. He is the Creator and Ruler of all things and the plans for living on the earth.

TEACHER: "And the power —"

They talked about different kinds of power: in waves, in seeds, winds, a growing baby, and in love.

JOHN C.: I wonder at the beauty of nature about us.

TEACHER: "And the glory forever —"

JOHN C.: God is worthy to be worshiped.

MARY BETH: God is forever.

TEACHER: "Amen." We ask that what we prayed for is in keeping with what God wants us to do.

PRAYER FOR CHILDREN IN A CLASS

Here is a portion of a fourth conversation about prayer in the fifth-grade class after it had done considerable thinking.

TEACHER: What is prayer?

JOHN C.: It is a time to think over the things you have done. It is talking with God.

JOHN A.: When you have done anything wrong, you want to correct it. You pray that God will help you correct it.

TEACHER: So prayer is also a time for asking God's forgiveness.

LARRY: When you pray, you are asking for God's guidance.

TEACHER: How do you think God guides us?

JOHN C.: He speaks through our conscience, our mind. Somehow you will know whether you have done wrong. Somehow we will know when something goes wrong.

LARRY: Yes, God has a way of making us know what to do through our conscience.

TEACHER: How else does God speak to us?

JOHN C.: Well, he also uses our fathers and mothers to help us know what to do. He speaks through our teachers, too.

TEACHER: Are there instances when you have felt that God was very near?

MARY BETH: O, yes. When I listen to the organ during our worship service, I feel God is so near me.

JOHN C.: Even the feel of the wind makes you wonder.

JOHN A.: When I go to bed at night and I think about the things I have done during the day, I feel God is close to me.

TEACHER: How do you feel when you are worshiping God?

JOHN C.: You feel so happy.

JOHN A.: You feel like helping somebody.

LARRY: Yes, you feel like doing something good for others. You just feel good inside.

JANE: You feel happy and thankful for the things you have enjoyed.

TEACHER: What have we discovered about worship from Jesus?

LARRY: When you pray, do not use empty words. Don't repeat words that do not mean anything to you.

MARY BETH: If you just repeat the prayer of another person, it is not so meaningful to you because it is not your own.

JOHN A.: When you pray, pray in private. You are talking to God, not to people.

JOHN C.: You can think better when you are alone and quiet. When you are in a group you may not be able to think your own thoughts.

LARRY: What about praying in church? It is not always quiet in church?

JOHN C.: When we sing, we are not making noise that disturbs worship.

TEACHER: I think Jesus was talking about people who prayed many times a day where they could be seen by other people.

JOHN C.: Giving should not be done to show off. It should be done quietly. If you give, do it generously.

MARY BETH: You should give with sincerity . . . Jesus said, "Before you give your offering, it is important that you settle your quarrel with your brother."

JOHN C.: You should not only say, "I'm sorry," but really sit down and talk things over. Then decide to be better friends.

JANE: Jesus said that we should forgive those who wrong us. If we don't forgive those who wrong us, God will not forgive us.

TEACHER: What does this mean?

JOHN C.: When we don't forgive those who wrong us, we do not feel right. We think bad thoughts. How then can we think about God's forgiveness? God is always forgiving us.

TEACHER: Yes, God's forgiveness is like a gift, always there ready for us. When we accept it, our attitude changes. We stop hating. We begin to love. When we love, we are able to forgive.

LEARNING TO PRAY IN MANY SITUATIONS

Since prayer or communication with God should grow into a continuous relationship, young folks may need to do much thinking about it in their classes in the church. Genuine prayer is not a mechanical saying of words and sounds or a vain repetition. Having in one's mind some worthy expressions of what one feels under varied circumstances may be helpful but such forms are not the end in prayer.

Chapter 19 contains some prayers created by children, particularly for use at mealtimes. These suggest the thinking that has led to their expression.

What are the situations outside of church where prayer may be involved? These can be thought about with children in their classes (as well as with their teachers and parents) and such prayers thought out cooperatively or individually may be recorded. Sometimes groups select the most varied and helpful ones to put into a booklet for all the class to keep and to refer to at home.

Some stanzas of hymns, appropriate for use at table, may be learned. The family may stand at their chairs and sing one of these before the meal or even at the close of it.

At the beginning of the day persons of many ages can think of God and how they may work with him that day. Perhaps a few memorized sentences to remind them of God will be helpful:

"O God, I give thee myself this day."

"Thanks be, O God, for your love and for your wonderful care of people."

"I will give thanks, O God, for you are good and for your wonderful love."

"O God, you are great and do wonderful things. Teach me your ways today."

"The earth is the Lord's . . . the world and those who live in it."

SITUATIONS FOR PRAYER

(1) When a child has done something wrong, he may need to learn how to think it over by himself with God on that very day. How did it affect the other person? Why did he do it? How can he make the situation better or even right? Here is an occasion for quiet thinking in the conscious presence of God. Is he ready to ask God's forgiveness and to do better?

(2) After seeing the vastness of the starry heavens, or watching an eclipse or some other impressive sight in the sky, there may be an occasion for prayer.

A teacher working with junior-age children in an institution found that evening prayer time was dull and thoughtless. After a conference on her problem, she decided to let all of them go to the window and look at the sky for a few minutes while she turned off the lights inside. They had a pleasant conversation and then she said, "We will speak to God here at the window tonight. You can speak out loud or quietly to God by yourself."

Soon, one of her troublesome boys said this:

"Dear God, I thank you for your wonderful world. Make me a good boy tomorrow." She believed this was a most meaningful prayer for him.

A poem, the right stanza of a hymn, or a few words of scripture by the parent may express the prayer for the child when he does not feel up to verbalization.

(3) On the death of a favorite pet or at the time of its burial, there is an occasion to recognize God. The fact that God planned for animals in his creation, the varied ways in which this pet has brought joy, the fun of caring for it, and numerous other things may lead to a prayer of thanksgiving.

Here is the occasion to avoid teaching that God planned to have it die or to be killed. Children need help on seeing God's big plan of life and how people have to work with it. Adults will do well to ponder *The Will of God,* by Leslie D. Weatherhead (Nashville: Abingdon Press, 1945) or *The Meaning of Suffering,* by Ralph Sockman (Nashville: Abingdon Press, 1962).

(4) Then there is the occasion of the death of a relative, a friend, or a neighbor. Many issues may need to be faced:

The importance of people's responsibility in helping others to be safe, in learning to heal them, and in caring for them properly are all aspects of the question.

The Christian belief in God's love for all people all the time and the fact that he never *plans* evil events must be faced. As one theologian says, not all things are the will of God, but his will is involved in every situation. How shall people work better with his plans?

Here is an occasion for children to learn that God is always present, even in the life of people whose bodies have ceased to function. Perhaps such a book as *Tell Me About Heaven (op. cit.)* or *Tell Me About God (op. cit.)*, both by Mary Alice Jones, will be useful on such occasions.

In many cases the prayers will be offered by parents or adults, and here they need to express thanksgiving for many of the good things enjoyed by the child in his relationships with the deceased person. The sense of God's presence as constant and continuous, even to the absent person, may also be involved in such prayers.

(5) Occasions when seeing great beauty may involve prayer. A stanza of "For the Beauty of the Earth" or "This Is My Father's World" or "All Creatures of Our God and King" may express the mood of prayer. The right selection of Scripture or poetry may be prayerful. Recognition of God as the creator of this plan for beauty may be expressed in thanksgiving and praise. Vivid, clear, brief sentences with one concrete fact in each are more significant than long ones full of abstraction. Praying means clear, sincere, definite thinking.

(6) A lakeside, a seaside, a mountaintop, a wooded scene, the marvel and beauty of flowers, and other natural settings may lead to the creation of vivid, clear, definite expressions of praise and thanksgiving to God as Creator. This is the occasion to recognize God.

Copernicus is said to have written:

To know the mighty works of God, to comprehend his wisdom and majesty and power; to appreciate in degree, the wonderful working of His laws, surely all this must be a pleasing and acceptable mode of worship to the Most High, to whom ignorance cannot be more grateful than knowledge.

(7) After preparing a gift for someone who is going away or for some people in an institution or for a faraway group (best for older children), there may be a prayer of appreciation for the people involved, and some expression of love and concern for them. Here is an occasion for cooperative think-

ing by the class, which can provide further benefits by putting some of the ideas on a large poster for all to see.

(8) A trip may become the subject of a prayer to be created by a class.

(9) Seeing a film or a live moth emerge can provide the occasion for creating of a prayer.

(10) A baby brought to a first grade may lead to praising God for the miracle of life, growth, and love as well as the importance of parents.

SOME PRAYERS CREATED BY CLASS GROUPS

OUR PSALM OF THANKS

O be thankful unto the Lord —
For the grass in the meadows,
For the flowers that give the bees honey,
For the beauty of the trees,
For the trees that give us our fruit.
He brings forth the sun, the moon, and the stars
And all the clouds in the sky.
He brings food from the grains of the field;
He sends the rains that help the crops grow.
He gave us the beautiful rivers,
The tall mountains covered with snow, and
The birds that sing songs.
For all the beauty of the earth
We thank thee.

— A junior class

GOD IS NEAR

Watching a squirrel build its nest
   Makes us feel that God is near and see his glory.
The sun rising over the lake
   Makes us feel that God is near and see his glory.
The stained-glass windows in St. Patrick's Cathedral
   Make us feel that God is near and see his glory.
The quiet lake in the early morning
   Makes us feel that God is near and see his glory.
A deer standing very still
   Makes us feel that God is near and see his glory.

Watching the ants building their home in an ant-house jar
    Makes us feel that God is near and see his glory.
The delicate petal of a ginger lily and its sweet fragrance
    Makes us feel that God is near and see his glory.
A carrier pigeon finding its way home
    Makes us feel that God is near and see his glory.
The bigness of the Gulf [of Mexico]
    Makes us feel that God is near and see his glory.
All things beautiful in sky or ground
    Make us feel that God is near and see his glory.

                        — *A sixth grade*

PRAYER TO THE GOD OF JESUS

O God, I like to think that the same bright sun which shines for us brought light and warmth to Jesus when he was a boy. I like to think that he saw the same bright stars in the great sky above us at night. I like to think that Jesus watched the same silver moon as he lay upon the roof of his house in Nazareth. O God, I am glad that you are the same great God who heard the prayers of Jesus when he prayed. Thank you for Jesus. Amen.

A PARAPHRASE OF THE LORD'S PRAYER

Almighty God, Father of all men, Creator and Ruler of the Universe, thy name be praised forever and be held in the highest reverence by all.

We would live according to thy will as Jesus taught and lived. May love rule our hearts and minds, that thy kingdom may come on earth. We would all work together to make the world a better place in which to live, that there may be better understanding of man and of thee; that there be peace, not war; and that everyone have the necessities of life.

We are sorry when we go against thy will. We would forgive those who injure us by what they say and what they do. Teach us to forgive them as thou dost forgive us, so that we may live in harmony with thee.

Let us not be tempted to forget thy commandments or to be turned away from thee. Give us strength to do the right whenever we think of doing wrong.

For all the universe, its power and glory belong to thee. Thy loving rule is the greatest, the mightiest of all powers. Thy love and goodness go on eternally. Thy way stands everlastingly as the true way. We would understand thee and live close to thee always. Amen.

                        — *A sophomore class*

ADOLESCENTS AND OLDER GROUPS LEARNING TO PRAY

There are many ways to help older groups deal with problems, questions, and the practice of prayer. Leaders will do well to review the chapters on prayer and on God in this volume, as well as such references as *More than We Are* by Margueritte H. Bro *(op. cit)*, and *Prayer and the Common Life* by Georgia Harkness *(op. cit.)*. These materials are, at best, *aids* to thinking about the meaning of prayer, because in one sense no one can teach another how to pray. Prayer is never a formal matter, but one of relationship and communication with God — vital, authentic, and personal. In a sense it is like love; it cannot be dictated but must grow within each individual. The teacher accepts these limitations, but recognizes that they still leave him free to lead his group in a variety of helpful ways.

Cultivating the awareness of God and his role in the universe, as well as the Christian comprehension of God's love, should help to produce a decision to accept his guidance and rule continuously.

Young people from twelve years and upwards, as well as adults, will have many questions and problems about prayer. Some will reveal enormous ignorance or even superstitions. These questions need to be listed on a big poster during a whole course of many sessions on prayer. Continuously the class should work to understand the nature of God as revealed at the highest in the Bible. God's relations to a universe that is beginning to expand in man's experience to an enormous degree must be recognized.

In a junior high class, the teacher asked, "Do you think God knows about atomic energy?" and the members agreed that he did not!

In the secular schools, much science is taught and experienced as if God were limited to church buildings or nonexistent. Prayer cannot develop well in such conditions. However, in the church environment, litanies, hymns, psalms, and more formal prayers of adoration, praise, and thanksgiving may well be created around events, observations, and experiences in the so-called material or physical world. A few situations may illustrate what is meant:

1. The discovery of Salk vaccine and what it means

2. The discovery of vaccine by Pasteur, his sacrificial persistence, its benefits to mankind, and its relation to God's order

3. Numerous discoveries which demonstrate God's physical and moral order and man's responsibility

4. Accidents and human failures

5. The problem of surplus foods in the U.S.A. while people in some parts of the world are hungry

6. Many ideas in Dr. Edmund W. Sinnott's fascinating book, *Matter, Mind, and Man* (New York: Harper & Row, 1957)

7. Processes used to help underdeveloped nations to provide food and health for their people

The study of the great prayers by other devoted Christians can be helpful. Some are included in the Appendix. Others will be found in Margueritte H. Bro's *Every Day a Prayer* (New York: Harper & Row, 1943).

When creating services of worship in a camp, the author has found it valuable to have several people work together over a period of weeks or days. Here is a unique and meaningful way to learn much about praying.

A group may also write and collect some helpful prayers and make a booklet for use in their group or for other young folks or older people.

Learning to pray at the beginning of the day, at mealtime, and at bedtime are occasions for thought and practice. Such questions as these are important:

How can we release our motives and wills to God for the day ahead?

In what manifold ways has God provided for our food and health? What is man's part?

What has been good about the day just finished? What have been one's failures and successes from God's perspective? How can we make right what was wrong? For what do we need forgiveness?

Children can begin to learn that prayer is based upon love and adoration of God and does not necessarily involve spoken words. It is a continuous awareness of God in all of life and an aspiration to accept his will at all times.[1]

[1] Teachers will gain great help at this point from *How to Pray*, by Jean-Nicholas Grou *(op cit.)*.

12.
Litanies and
Responsive Readings

IT HAS BEEN FOUND OVER A PERIOD OF YEARS that the litany is an effective way for older children and young people to express prayer and also to participate in worship. The word "litany" comes from a Greek verb which means "to pray." The litany is a very old form of congregational participation. The reformers in Germany dropped it from their worship, but in recent years there has been a return to its use. The litany may express penitence, but more often its modern use expresses joy and praise.

There are limitations in the use and value of this form of responsive participation. Attention is usually best focused when the litany is short, and particularly when it is placed at a point in the service where the people have faced some concrete data which leads to the prayer. It is unwise to use involved sentences, polysyllabic words, or assonance. The leaders should read the materials aloud to discover any pitfalls in the reading. Petitions and responses in the litany should be short. Usually the same short response for the congregation is used after each prayer until the last when the response may be slightly longer. These responses may be said or sung.

Children's Litanies

The litany lends its use to worship by children and young people, particularly when their own groups have created the litany as the climax and outgrowth of some long unit of study or some significant experience. These litanies may be used in "climax programs" and to close a series of worship services or on special days.

Young folks may have remarkable experiences in learning to pray and in expressing prayers when a group works with its leader in deciding upon major ideas and ways of expressing these in prayer. Usually it is wise to decide early upon the response to be sung or said so as to create the prayer in a suitable form to precede it.

The following litanies reveal something of the experiences out of which they grew:

LITANY OF THANKSGIVING

For water to drink,
For food to eat,
Father in heaven, we thank you.

For clothes to keep us warm,
For boots and rubbers to keep us dry,
Father in heaven, we thank you.

For our mothers who cook our food,
For our fathers who work to buy it,
Father in heaven, we thank you.

For our church we love so well,
For its help when there is need,
Father in heaven, we thank you.

— *A fourth-grade class*

LITANY OF APPRECIATION

For the laws of growth, the seed time and the harvest,
O God, we thank thee.

For the seasons, the sun, the rain, the snow, the dew, and the warm winds,
We thank thee, God.

For beauty in color and the fragrance of blossoms, for Luther Burbank and others who labored to produce new loveliness,

We are glad this day.

For men and women whose study and experimentation have improved the quality and increased the quantity of food products; for Patrick Sheriff, David Fife, Dr. Charles Saunders, who improved wheat, and for countless other farmers,

We thank thee, God.

For scientists and teachers who use their time and talent to help the gardeners of the world,

We are grateful, O God.

LITANY OF THANKS FOR GOD'S LOVE WORKING IN PEOPLE

O God, we are learning about your world, and, as we study, we keep finding you at work in it. Where people are crowded together in the city, we find men like Jacob Riis trying to make things better. We find women like Jane Addams, trying to make people happier. For these men and women,

We thank you, God.

Where great ships land, bringing people from other countries, we find friendly teachers who try to make the first days here pleasant. Where our guests from far away might be lonely, we find places where they may live together and make friends; for International House,

We thank you, God.

Where people are homesick for books which they can understand and read, we find libraries with shelves and shelves of books written in many languages, and we find rooms where even the blind may read. For the friendly thought which built our library,

We thank you, God.

Where children need love and care, we find homes like the Sheltering Arms. For the helpers in these homes,

We thank you, God.

For policemen who care for the helpless, for doctors and nurses who care for the sick, for all those who are working with you to make a safer, happier world.

We thank you, God.

And now may your spirit be with us, oh God. We know there is much yet to do. Help us to remember that you are depending on us to make this world still better. Amen.

— A primary class

LITANY OF THE LORD'S PRAYER

Our Father who art in heaven,

Who loves everyone and creates beautiful things for us, and who is greater than we can imagine him to be; may we observe the beauty and love in everything.

Hallowed be thy name.

Honored and glorified and just is thy name in all the earth.

Thy kingdom come, thy will be done on earth as it is in heaven.

The earth is full of beauty, goodness, truth, and love. We would plan and work and do our best to help God to do the rest, with the strength that he gives to us. Let thy kingdom of love flow through us. So guide us that we will want to fulfill thy purposes.

Give us this day our daily bread.

Fill us with the desire to share the bread with others who lack food and also to share thy word of salvation.

And forgive us our debts as we forgive our debtors.

We must forgive. We must forget. These are hard things. Yet God forgives and forgets. He has not lost his kingdom yet. To be like God is our aim. So let us forgive as many times as we need to. We are safe and we are sane.

And lead us not into temptation, but deliver us from evil,

God gave us minds with which to think and to make our own choices — right or wrong. It takes self-control to do the right things. He will clean all our evil thoughts if we obey his word. Our lives are his and his alone. He shall deliver. He shall save. Let us praise the God of grace.

For thine is the kingdom and the power and the glory, forever,

For thou didst make this kingdom on earth and all the living things which are in it and it is thine. And the power which thou didst build out of, and the glory which thou didst put in it are also thine, forever and ever. God is the ruler. No power can overtake him. He alone is to be glorified. No earthly thing must be placed in our hearts for worship. Let us praise him.

Amen.

May it be as we have prayed. May we help to bring this prayer

to pass by doing what we have promised to do. *May we wake up to the realization of thy goodness. Amen.*

— An eighth-grade class

LITANY OF NATURE

The sun wakes us in the morning.
It keeps us warm
And helps us to grow strong.
The sun helps leaves to grow
And makes our food.

God planned it so. Thank you, God, for the sun.

The sun helps flowers to grow,
And green grass.
The sun shines on the birds;
It makes our world beautiful.

God planned it so. Thank you, God, for the sun.

When we plant seeds in the earth,
The roots go down to find water.
The leaves reach up toward the sun.
The sun helps the leaves to make food,
So that the plant may grow.

God planned it so. Thank you, God, for the sun.

After the leaves, come the flowers —
Yellow or blue or white,
Purple or pink or red.

God planned it so. Thank you, God, for the sun.

The flowers drop off, and then
Fruit comes.
When we look inside the fruit
We find the seeds,
And a new plant begins to grow.

God planned it so. Thank you, God, for the sun.

— A primary class taught by Margaret Wallace at Seaside Sanatorium

LITANY OF BEAUTIFUL THINGS

God giveth us richly all things to enjoy.
For red roses and yellow tulips that grow in the flower garden,

We thank you, God, for all beautiful things.

For daisies and lilies that grow in the fields,

We thank you, God, for all beautiful things.

For trees with branches that wave in the wind,

We thank you, God, for all beautiful things.

For pointed pine trees that stay green all winter.

We thank you, God, for all beautiful things.

For bluebirds and robins, pheasants and red-winged blackbirds, scarlet tanagers and goldfinches and orioles that sing in the morning.

We thank you, God, for all beautiful things.

For the blue brook that trickles over the rocks,

We thank you, God, for all beautiful things.

For the ocean and the waves that rock back and forth and wash onto the shore,

We thank you, God, for all beautiful things.

For the stars that sparkle in the night,

We thank you, God, for all beautiful things.

For the moon that is sometimes like a ball and sometimes only half a ball,

We thank you, God, for all beautiful things.

— A primary class

A LITANY OF THANKS

God, you planned the day,
The night, the stars, the moon, the seas, and the mountains.

We give thanks unto thee, O God.

You planned the earth,
And you planned for sun and rain to make the seeds grow.

We give thanks unto thee, O God.

God, you planned the spring with cool breezes and flowers,
The summer with green trees and beaming sun,
The fall with red and yellow and brown leaves,
The winter with snow and ice
To follow each other, always the same.

We give thanks unto thee, O God.

You planned each little seed to look different on the outside,
But all are alike on the inside,
Since in each one is something that gives it life.

We give thanks unto thee, O God.

And God, you have planned for us.

We give thee thanks, especially for your plan for us. Amen.

— A primary class

LITANY OF THANKS FOR FREEDOM

We are thankful, God,

For men like Thomas Hooker, George Fox, William Penn, and Lord Baltimore who believed so strongly in religious freedom that they were willing to suffer in order that others could live together with understanding,

We are glad, God,

That we have been able to learn more about how to live with people of other races and religions,

We are thankful, God,

That we have a chance to help others in understanding people who believe differently than we do,

We believe, God,

That sometime all people may find true religious freedom,

For all these things, we are thankful, God.

LITANY OF PENITENCE

Because we have built our society upon greed and selfish desire for gain,

Forgive us and save us, O Lord.

Because we have glorified wealth, fortified the rich, and browbeaten the poor,

Forgive us and save us, O Lord.

From the arrogance and conceit which have caused us, when we have prospered, to believe ourselves special recipients of the favor of God,

Deliver and save us from our sins.

Because we as the church of Jesus Christ have been too often dominated by the desire for material gain and success as the business world,

Forgive us and save us from this sin.

Because we have not always entered into the sufferings of the poor and dispossessed of this earth; because we have often failed to share vicariously their mental anguish, their hunger, their broken spirit,

We beseech thee in mercy to forgive us.

Because we have assumed the standards set by Jesus Christ to be impossible, and therefore refused to meet them in our own conduct,

We beseech thee to forgive us and lead us into a new and full acceptance of him.

RESPONSIVE PRAYER (SIMILAR TO A LITANY)

Great, O God, is our need of thee, greater than we know, far greater than we can say.

Our minds need thee to give them poise.

Our wills need thee to give them strength.

Our hearts need thee to bring them comfort and give them peace.

We need thee every morning, when we go forth to labor.

We need thee at noonday, when we stand where cross the crowded ways of life.

We need thee at eventide, when the darkness deepens and we find ourselves alone with our fears and hopes and aspirations.

We need thee in sorrow, to keep us from giving way to despair.

We need thee in joy, to prevent our yielding to selfishness.

We need thee when we are sick, in order that we may recover our strength.

We need thee when we are well, in order that we may apply our strength to noble ends.

O thou merciful Father of us all, grant unto us now a blessed consciousness of thy presence, that this may become indeed a holy day.

LITANY FOR WASHINGTON'S BIRTHDAY

In a time of hesitation and trembling,
When old standards seem to be slipping,
When ancient foundations appear unstable,
When we grope for certainty,

Raise up for a free people, O Lord, leaders whom we may confidently follow.

In a time of eager questioning,
When traditions are lightly regarded,
When youth insists upon creating its own institutions,
When the counsels of the fathers are easily rejected,

Raise up for a free people, O Lord, leaders whom we may confidently follow.

In a time when the novel fascinates,
When the old ways no longer charm,
When the glitter of the surface is alluring,
When the last herald of panaceas cries most loudly,

Raise up for a free people, O Lord, leaders whom we may confidently follow.

LITANY OF THE KINGDOM OF GOD

O God, who hast made all things by thy power, thou King and Ruler of the world, glorious in beauty and truth and love,

Thine is the kingdom and the power and the glory, forever and ever.

O God, who hast shown us the glory of thy kingdom in the dreams of the prophets, and in the majestic love of Jesus Christ,

Thine is the kingdom and the power and the glory, forever and ever.

O God, who art ever working in the world by thy mighty and creative Spirit, to manifest thy kingdom among men,

Thine is the kingdom and the power and the glory, forever and ever.

O God, who hast made man that he should be the praise of thy glory,

Thine is the kingdom and the power and the glory, forever and ever.

O God, who hast given our wills that we may offer them to thee,

Thine is the kingdom and the power and the glory, forever and ever.

O God, whose kingdom is where thy will is done, and the service of whose will is perfect freedom.

Thine is the kingdom and the power and the glory, forever and ever.

O God, whose will is power, and in the doing of whose will men are endued with power from on high,

Thine is the kingdom and the power and the glory, forever and ever.

O God, who dost will that, through the service of men in fellowship with thy will, thine age-long purpose for all the peoples of the earth shall be fulfilled,

Thine is the kingdom and the power and the glory, forever and ever.

O God, who hast set before us the great hope that thy kingdom shall be established upon earth, so rule our lives by thy Spirit that all our thoughts, desires, and acts, being made obedient unto thee, thy power, thy glory, and the mightiness of thy kingdom, may be made known unto men; grant this, O merciful Father, for thy great love's sake.

Amen.

A GENERAL LITANY

Almighty God, Creator of the boundless universe, who art still near to the humblest, struggling human soul that calls upon thee, we thank thee for thy continued presence in our minds and hearts, making us ever discontent with things as they are, and urging us ever forward and upward on our way. For exalted visions of the eternal destiny of man, and for the dreams of a divine society on earth, foretold by prophets throughout the centuries, and proclaimed by Jesus in the glad tidings of the kingdom of God,

We thank thee, our Father.

For our failure to be stirred by the voice within us, and by the need around us, and the vision of the kingdom of the future; for our selfish willingness to accept comfort and privilege and security, while others around us suffer hunger and tragedy, loneliness and despair,

We pray thy forgiveness, O God.

That we may see with clearer vision where love of ease and privilege, or cowardice, has kept us from saying, "Here am I; send me!"

We earnestly beseech thee, O God.

To the call of the needs of the world which thou canst not redeem apart from us,

We dedicate ourselves, O God.

To the search for some definite part which each of us can play, a concrete step to take in helping to meet some one of the great unfinished tasks of the kingdom of God,

We dedicate ourselves, O God.

O Lord, make us instruments of thy peace. Where there is hatred, let us sow love; where there is injury, pardon; where there is discord, union; where there is doubt, faith; where there is darkness, light; where there is sadness, joy. Amen.

— St. Francis of Assisi (adapted)

A LITANY OF THANKS FOR JESUS

For Jesus, who believed in men to the last and through all disappointment never completely lost heart,

We thank thee, O God.

Who carried obedience to God to the point of death, even death on the cross, and remained faithful to the end,

We thank thee, O God.

Who taught men to love their enemies, who was good and kind and helped people in need, who treated all men as brothers and always believed that there was some good in everyone,

We thank thee, O God.

For the disciples of Jesus who, because of their faithfulness, have continued Jesus' loving way,

We thank thee, O God.

For the spirit of Jesus which did not die but still lives in the hearts of many people today as they continue his work in the world,

We thank thee, O God.

For the opportunity to live the good life that Jesus taught, in order that we may radiate the good news that God's love is eternal, and that he who loves can never die,

We thank thee, O God.

RESPONSIVE READINGS

Responsive readings resemble litanies in the somewhat superficial characteristic that the leader and the group participate alternately in the various parts. The responsive reading, however, is often based on Scripture, is not a prayer, and does not use the device of repetition.

Growing out of a long study of Jesus, a group of seventh-grade students prepared a climax worship program. They told the story of the religion of Jesus in slides along with a story of the ongoingness of Jesus' life. The class prepared a responsive reading, using the King James Version of the New Testament, to follow the story:

Jesus taught us about prayer:
And when thou prayest, thou shalt not be as the hypocrites are: for they love to pray standing in the synagogues and in the corners of the streets, that they may be seen of men. Verily I say unto you, They have their reward.

> *But thou, when thou prayest, enter into thy closet, and when thou hast shut thy door, pray to thy Father which is in secret; and thy Father which seeth in secret shall reward thee openly.*

But when ye pray, use not vain repetitions, as the heathen do: for they think that they shall be heard for their much speaking.

> *Be not ye therefore like unto them, for your Father knoweth what things ye have need of before ye ask him.*

Jesus taught and expressed love:
The Lord our God is one Lord.

> *And thou shalt love the Lord thy God with all thy heart, and with all thy soul, and with all thy mind, and with all thy strength: this is the first commandment.*

And the second is like, namely this, Thou shalt love thy neighbor as thyself. There is none other commandment greater than these.

> *A new commandment I give unto you, That ye love one another; as I have loved you, that ye also love one another.*

By this shall all men know that ye are my disciples, if ye have love one to another.

Jesus expressed love to people and changed them:
And, behold, there was a man named Zaccheus, which was the chief among the publicans, and he was rich.

> *And he sought to see Jesus who he was; and could not for the press, because he was of little stature. And he ran before, and climbed up into a sycomore tree to see him: for he was to pass that way.*

And when Jesus came to the place, he looked up and saw him, and said unto him, Zaccheus, make haste, and come down; for today I must abide at thy house. And he made haste, and came down; and received him joyfully.

> *And when they saw it, they all murmured saying, That he was gone to be a guest with a man that is a sinner.*

And Zaccheus stood, and said unto the Lord: Behold, Lord, the half of my goods I give to the poor; and if I have taken anything from any man by false accusation, I restore him fourfold.

And Jesus said unto him, This day is salvation come to this house.

Jesus had faith in God:

And why take ye thought for raiment? Consider the lilies of the field, how they grow; they toil not, neither do they spin. And yet I say unto you, That even Solomon in all his glory was not arrayed like one of these.

Wherefore, if God so clothe the grass of the field, which today is, and tomorrow is cast into the oven, shall he not much more clothe you . . . ?

Therefore take no thought, saying, What shall we eat? or, What shall we drink? or, Wherewithal shall we be clothed? for your heavenly Father knoweth that ye have need of all these things.

But seek ye first the kingdom of God, and his righteousness; and all these things shall be added unto you.

13.
Worship Through Music

ATTENDING SERVICES OF WORSHIP and saying a memorized prayer at night are usually not adequate as means of learning to worship. Time should be set aside to study the meaning of prayer, suitable concepts of God, a vital relationship to God, procedures in orderly worship, of hymns, introits, and responses, and many other elements, together with their use in worship. Most important is suitable hymnology.

PROBLEMS IN THE CHOICE OF HYMNS

In the 1930's, Elsa Lotz made a considerable study, while in the Hartford School of Religious Education, of favorite hymns and their meaning. In all, over 6,000 hymns were reported. It is impossible here to give a total listing, but it is clear from an examination of these titles that the hymns did not reflect much intelligent discrimination as to the quality of poetry, music, or the religious content. Often there was a lack of standards of value. No marked differences could be detected among the denominations as to the quality of the hymns chosen. There were absurd, confused, and meaningless ideas of God.

Many of the favorite hymns were not addressed to God; in fact only a small percentage were. There were numerous "I," "me," and "my" choices.

In trying to determine the reason for hymn preference, the study revealed that associations in early childhood and in summer assemblies rated highest in their effects. Religious education may well learn from this the importance of more work with families as well as with teachers and leaders of children and young folks. The impression of hymns seems to depend in no small measure on the occasion, the associations, and the manner in which they are introduced.

Comments by some of the more discriminating adult respondents are suggestive for the educator in worship.

"Certain hymns I dislike because of the false interpretation of God they suggest, and other theological ideas which to me are false or misleading."

"Let us have more hymns and fewer 'jingles' in our worship."

"I like hymns that help me to a better understanding of God."

"There is need for new hymns related to life around us and to God."

"Sense and nonsense and medieval superstition are so confused in much Christmas music as to destroy its real value."

"I like hymns that emphasize God's fatherly care over all nature and God's interest in all works."

"In hymns I generally like the notes of appreciation of the divine love, a call to service for others, a sense of fellowship with others in devotion and service, a universal note, and a courageous facing of life."

"I like the hymns that best express the oneness of mankind, the love of and need for God, and the spirit of cooperation and brotherhood."

"I like 'Gather Us In' because it shows a broad conception of God and humanity and because it includes all races and religious denominations as children of God, the same God that the soul craves under whatever names we call him."

"I like 'These Things Shall Be' because it does not ask for selfish things, and does not give commands to God."

These comments by a few discriminating respondents are suggestive of some of the elements involved in building up higher standards in taste and the choice of hymns.

THE PSYCHOLOGY OF HYMNS

Kimball Young in his study, *The Psychology of Hymns*,[1] says that social pressures in the form of negative attitudes surround us from infancy, leaving infantile and primitive impulses in behavior patterns. From these develop neuroses, dreams, or strange social forms. An emotional release which might otherwise create social difficulties is provided by religious rituals.

Intense religious expression can emerge from a crowd situation and the shoulder-to-shoulder movement of the emotional appeal of rhythmic hymns.

Young used nearly three thousand simple hymns to make his study. In these hymns there was repetition, *plain* phrasing and emotional stimulation.

In summary, the reaction to some hymns represented a return to childhood identification with one's parents, and so projected an image of God, compensation for unfulfilled wishes by reward, satisfaction and joy by being at one with God in victory over death and sin, pleasure in pain by love for the Savior, and release of impulses in symbolic form related to a sense of quiet caused by social pressures.

From such symbols and religious formulations, said Young, "improvements will grow out of more adequate unconscious adjustments of our instincts, emotions, and intellect to the world of reality which surrounds us."

[1] Kimball Young, "The Psychology of Hymns," in the *Journal of Abnormal and Social Psychology*, Vol. 20, 1926, pp. 391ff.

Learning from the Past

The place and kind of music used in the church over nineteen centuries is an amazing history. In the early times the song was a chant or recitative. It conformed to the meter and accent of the text. Perhaps this practice grew out of the ancient Hebrew chant. After intoning each verse or portion of a chant, hymn, or prayer, a chorus of high voices (probably young boys) responded to a chorus of men's voices.

Psalms were intoned by the leader, a half-verse at a time, and repeated by the congregation, the leader singing each succeeding half-line and pausing for the response so the congregation was drawn into the worship service.

The early Christians expressed their religious joy in music, some of which was composed by their own membership. Moods of praise and prayer came from the Psalms and other portions of the Old Testament. Religious education took place through the content of the music. We read of Bar Daisan of Edessa (A.D. 150-222) writing one hundred fifty psalms to sing between the biblical Psalms in the service of the Syriac Church.

Gradually the clergy, who seem to have been trained in chanting, took over the music from the laity. The liturgy grew more elaborate. At first there was antiphonal singing between people and clergy, until finally the clergy took it over entirely. Then the antiphonal was between the priests and the choir, who stood behind the altar. Sometimes this choir was made up of lesser clergy.

In the development of the mass, music came to be used to enhance its drama and solemnity, in combination with lights, vestments, and clouds of incense which led the mind into a mood of adoration. The mass was a sacrifice; it was worship.

Vespers and other services of worship demanded many forms of music. In this history of the church we feel the dramatic quality of the services and their appeal to the congregation, many of whom were illiterate.

The great royal chapel of the fifteenth century spread over Europe, and became a tremendously important influence on church music.

Palestrina (1526-1594) created with great art ninety masses, and the plainsong, introducing calmness, exultation, and eternal repose, freeing the music from profane suggestion.

During the reformation, more attention was given to the people's part in worship. Language was made that of the congregation. John Hus encouraged this movement by writing hymns in the Czech language.

Then came Martin Luther, who condemned medieval ceremonial and over-elaborate music as found in the Latin church. He began early to write metrical hymns and psalms, and set them to music within the reach of the congregation so that even the rudest could share. Later Luther created hymns for the people of his time and dealt with the ideas and conflicts of his period. These hymns emphasized the new religious beliefs. Old introits were translated into the language of the people. The creed was sung during the communion while even the Epistle and the Gospel were sung in German.

In Zurich (1525) music was abolished for a time, and the recitation of psalms and canticles was substituted. Later on, congregational singing was introduced.

One of the oldest Protestant denominations is that of the Moravians, who finally made their way to America. Music and hymnody were an important part of their religious life. They created many forms including the chorale. They sang on all occasions—at work, at mealtime, and in worship; music was a continuous response.

The English church, after Henry VIII broke with the church at Rome, brought a rich musical contribution to the worship service, much of which was rendered in musical form. Sentences, antiphonals, prayers and collects, and the litany were chanted by the priest. The creed was sung, and there was much antiphonal participation by the congregation.

Calvin influenced the Scottish church. He had declared that "all that is needed is a simple and pure singing of the divine praises, coming from heart and mouth, and in the vulgar tongue." In the Calvin and Knox service books, the people expressed adoration, thanksgiving, and praise solely in metrical psalms. These constituted the Scottish music. Such influences were reflected by the Puritans, who prohibited all hymns except paraphrases of the Psalms.

Congregational singing decayed in the American churches until finally singing schools were established to help the people to learn how to sing in the churches.

In the nineteenth century a powerful contribution to congregational singing was made by the Wesleys, who created many fervent lyrics. Charles Wesley taught Christian doctrine through his hymns, which became a source of inspiration and power in the religious meetings of his brother John.

Within the last four decades considerable attention has been given to hymnbooks for adults as well as for young people in the American Protestant churches. More recognition of liturgy by the many nonconformist churches has revived the use of varied kinds of church music, particularly older forms.

Some attention has been given to the writing of hymns suited to the idiom and life of the present age, but not nearly enough. Better expression of religious and theological meanings suited to this age is needed. Many stanzas, as well as whole hymns, could well be deleted from our hymn books. Just as Martin Luther wrote hymns for his people, able writers need to create more for our age.

Young people and adult laymen need far greater education in the history of worship and of hymnody. Perspective comes when we see the whole pattern of our inheritance.

Music in our services still needs to instruct appropriately and to enhance the experience of worship. This task involves far more unity in the creation of services of worship and the placing of music so that it meets the need of the worshiper in each particular part of the service. Worship services are not the occasion for singing popular choices, either for exercise or for drill. Movement God-ward by the worshiper is all-important. Great music of religious import, good poetry, and meaningful content in hymnody still constitute an important aspect of religious vision and growth for all worshipers.

In the hymnody of the past there are works of art. When within the range of their worship experiences, some of these should become familiar to juniors, intermediates, and seniors. Through periods set aside for worship training great progress can be made in gloriously singing the music in the worship. Far more effort is needed to prepare all who worship to participate in the service and particularly in the singing.

Elements in Good Hymnology

In teaching religious songs and hymns to children and young people there are several elements to keep in mind:

1. The music should have a religious association and suit the words and their meaning.

2. The harmony in general should not attract attention to the chords (diatonic, not chromatic). Many Victorian hymns *overuse* chromatic harmony and thus weaken the melody. A limited use of chromaticism is necessary for legitimate modulation; in fact Bach is a chromaticist in his harmonizations.

3. The rhythm must be suited to the subject and capable of lifting the worshiper.

4. The melody should be suitable. In general, it should be principally in step-wise progression. "Toulon" illustrates this step-wise progression. A good tune normally covers about an octave; the low, and particularly the high point, usually occurring only once in the middle of the melody, as in "Land of Rest" and "Austria." There are some great hymns which do not follow stepwise movement, such as "St. Anne" and

"Frankfort." The use of skips within the chord may form legitimate melody. Usually we should avoid difficult slurs in the music of children.

5. As a *general rule,* triple meters (3/4, 3/2) are not so strong as duple and quadruple meters (2/4, 2/2, 4/4, 4/2). A problem lies in the use of the triple rhythm of the composer by the organist or pianist. There are fine hymn tunes in triple rhythm: "In Dulci Jubilo," "Hyfrydol," "King's Weston," and "Martyrdom." There is a place for some irregular meters with older children and adolescents, as in the plainsong tunes and in metrical psalm tunes, and some contemporary ones. For juniors and older young people, "All Creatures of Our God and King" deserves to be learned.

6. Avoid scale steps or skips that follow the same pattern. Watch for variety and balance.

7. The words should be genuinely religious in feeling, not merely theological.

8. Words and music should be joyous.

9. Words should have genuine poetic value.

10. The content of the hymn should have unity, coherence, and emphasis.

11. The concepts of God should be worthy and Christian.

12. The mood and ideas should be suitable for praising to God.

13. The language should be meaningful to the worshiper, for it is he who is being led in the worship of God.

14. The content should be worthy of being expressed in sincerity by the worshiper. This involves the finest in music, poetry, and thought. Avoid the trivial both in music and content.

15. The concepts should be acceptable for the age group using them and should be those which can become permanent in his religious growth. (For example, avoid locating God in the sky).

16. The content of the hymn should fit into present-day experiences and living and give direction to them.

17. Music of strictly historical value should be reserved for settings of drama or for special occasions. See *The English Carol* by Erik Routley (New York: Oxford University Press, 1958).

MUSIC MATERIALS FOR DIFFERENT AGES

It is doubtful whether genuine hymns are useful much before six years of age. Younger children will find great joy in rhythmic activities and in singing about their near-at-hand activities and experiences.

Nursery

Among the finest of the resources for preschool children are Satis N. Coleman and Alice G. Thorn's *Singing Time* (New York: John Day Co., 1929) and *Another Singing Time* (New York: John Day Co., 1937).

Kindergarten

At the kindergarten age, some of the previous materials may also be used and particularly *The Martin and Judy Songs* by Edith Lovell Thomas (*op. cit.*). A superb guide for the teacher is *Music in the Church Kindergarten,* by Phyllis Maramarco (Hartford: Connecticut Council of Churches).

Primary

Children at six years of age can begin gradually to learn how to worship more formally. These children and those of the next two grades will find much material to use in Jeanette P. Brown's *As Children Worship* (Philadelphia: United Church, 1936) and Edith L. Thomas's *Sing, Children Sing,* (*op. cit.*).

Junior

At the junior age level, many useful hymns may be found in Jeannette P. Brown's *Children's Worship in the Church*

School (New York: Harper & Row, 1939), in *Hymns for Junior Worship* (Philadelphia: Westminster Press, 1940), and in Edith Lovell Thomas's *Singing Worship with Boys and Girls* (Nashville: Abingdon Press, 1958).

Adolescent

At the adolescent age level many more good choices of hymn books are available. Excellent taste is particularly prevalent in *Beacon Song and Service Book* (Boston: Beacon Press, 1960) and *At Worship: A Hymnal for Young Churchmen*, by Roy A. Burkhart & others (New York: Harper & Row, 1951). For all ages considerable material is available in *The Whole World Singing*, by Edith Lovell Thomas (New York: Friendship Press, 1950). The songs come from many lands with ballads and chants. This sort of music is of particular interest to this age-group.

College

For the college age there is the *Hymnal for Colleges and Schools* by E. Harold Geer (New Haven: Yale University Press, 1956).

Some Special Children's Hymns

For Primary Ages

SURPRISES

O dear God, I love your surprises in spring!
1. Today I found a tiny yellow flower
   Lifting its head from the ground.
2. This morning on my lawn
   I heard a robin bursting in song.
3. Outside my window I can see
   The new green leaves on our apple tree.
4. And my "Thank you," "Thank you," "Thank you,"
   Is the melody that I sing.
O dear God, I love your surprises in spring.[2]

[2] By William Crotch. From *Thoughts of God for Boys and Girls* (*op. cit.*). Used by permission of the Connecticut Council of Churches. Set to music by Edith L. Thomas in *Sing, Children, Sing* (*op. cit.*).

BLESSINGS ON EFFORT

'Tis God our Heav'nly Father,
Who makes each little seed,
And puts away within it,
The tiny plant we need.
And then he leaves us our part,
To seek that plant within,
So when we add our work to his,
We find what is therein.

Man ploughs the field and scatters,
The wheat seed all around.
But 'tis God who sends the sunlight,
And rain upon the ground.
He sends his rain and sunshine,
To help to make our bread.
And when we add our work to his,
The hungry can be fed.[3]

GOD'S CHILDREN LIVE IN MANY LANDS

God's children live in many lands,
All scattered wide and far,
Where nights are long and snow is deep
Beneath the northern star;
Where flowers bloom, where rivers roll,
Where mountains tower high;
But all with one old earth for home,
And under one blue sky.

Chorus

Touch hands around the rolling world,
Call clear, from sea to sea,
That brothers, sisters are we all
In God's great family!
God's children speak in different tongues,
With different things to say,
And different tasks and different toys,
And many a different way;

---

[3] From *Song Stories for the Sunday School* by Patty S. Hill and Mildred J. Hill (Chicago: Clayton F. Summy Company, 1899).

[4] From *Song and Play for Children* by Frances W. Danielson and Grace W. Conant (Boston: Pilgrim Press, 1953). Used by permission.

And some are dark, and some are fair,
And some are scarcely known;
But each is kin to all the rest,
And each the Father's own.[4]

For Juniors

"For Man's Unceasing Quest for God," by Alice M. Pullen.
"Glad Let Us Be," words by Doris M. Gill; music by Alice
M. Pullen.

For Adolescent and Older Groups

In Chapter 17 will be found a classified list of suggested
hymns and introits for varied use. The following books will
be found rich with suggestions:

Burkhart, Roy A. and others, *At Worship: A Hymnal for Young
Churchmen*. New York: Harper & Row, 1951.
Davison, Archibald T., *Church Music, Illusion and Reality*. Cam-
bridge: Harvard University Press, 1952.
Dearmer, Percy, ed., *Oxford Book of Carols*. New York: Oxford
University Press, 1928.
Lovelace, Austin and Rice, William, *Music and Worship in the
Church*. Nashville: Abingdon Press, 1960.
Pilgrim Hymnal. Boston: Pilgrim Press, 1958. A very rich collec-
tion of hymnody.
Routley, Erik, *Church Music and Theology*. Philadelphia: For-
tress Press, 1960.
——————, *The English Carol*. New York: Oxford University
Press, 1958.

Much in the above-listed applies to the adult service of
worship, but they also deserve special study by workers with
adolescents and juniors.

If the service is brief the hymns may be limited to one —
after the prayer. Here are a few that are important:

"All Creatures of Our God and King"
"Faith of Our Fathers"
"Gather Us In" (by George Matheson)
"God Send Us Men"
"Good Christian Men, Rejoice" (Tune: Gelobt sei Gott)
"In Christ There Is No East or West"

"Joyful, Joyful, We Adore Thee"
"Lord of All Being" (Tune: Uffingham)
"Lord of the Sunlight" [5]
"Now Thank We All Our God"
"O Beautiful for Spacious Skies"
"O God, Whose Love Is Over All"
"O Young and Fearless Prophet" (by Ralph Harlow)
"The Spacious Firmament on High"
"These Things Shall Be"
"We Thank Thee, O Our Father"
"We Would Be Building" (Tune: Finlandia)
"Where Cross the Crowded Ways of Life"

How to Teach Hymns and Songs

(1) Do not teach hymns in a formal worship service. Instead, on some occasions, use the entire worship period to study hymns and other ingredients of worship. Several sessions a month for this purpose would not be too many, especially at the beginning of the season. After the rehearsal, close with a suitable prayer. In camps and vacation schools a whole period may be used daily for training in worship.

(2) For children who are beginning to read, the words of songs and hymns can be printed on posters and hung on a chart-rack made for the purpose. It should be high enough to be read by those in the rear seats. In this way more things can be in process of learning, fewer books are needed, unusual materials can be taught, and all heads lifted up to sing.

(3) Sing the stanza as a whole, not line by line. To introduce a hymn, someone may sing it while the boys' and girls' eyes are on the words.

(4) Discuss the *main thought* of the song and interpret unfamiliar words.

(5) Use only the melody in the first stages of teaching a song or hymn to children, adding the harmony after the melody is thoroughly learned. With younger children it is

[5] No. 28 in *Sing, Children, Sing*, by Edith Lovell Thomas (Nashville: Abingdon Press, 1939).

well to teach songs without using any instrument other than the human voice.

(6) Repeat the singing several times until the children feel a satisfaction in having learned the song.

(7) One or two pictures may help children to build suitable associations with a hymn.

(8) Review the new hymns and songs frequently. When they have been properly learned, use them in worship services.

(9) Aim to make the learning of a hymn a worshipful experience.

CREATING HYMNS

Under able teachers, young folks may create some hymns. These will relate to the experiences of a group and become particularly meaningful. Two such hymns follow.

THIS WE KNOW

This we know: Spring will follow winter snow;
After night the sun will show, and from tiny seeds
Bright flowers grow;
This we know: God's love goes on and on and on,
And in a loving heart will ever glow.

WE EXPLORE

We explore to discover new things in the world.
Man long ago discovered fire,
He began to talk and to defend himself
He thought that there was more than one god,
In water, sky, fire, and tree.
We explore to discover new things in the world.
People today use fire in stoves,
Talk on telephones and ride in aeroplanes.
We know that there is only one God;
He is a loving and a kind God.
We explore to discover new things in the world.[6]

---

[6] These two hymns are used by permission of the late Phyllis N. Maramarco, former Director of Children's Work, Connecticut Council of Churches.

PART TWO: RESOURCES AND SERVICES

14.
Worship Bibliography

TO EXAMINE YOUR OWN IDEA OF WORSHIP

Baxter, Edna M., *How Our Religion Began*. New York: Harper & Row, 1939. Being revised.

Bowman, Clarice M., *The Living Art of Worship*. New York: Association Press, 1964.

Casteel, John L., *Renewal in Retreats*. New York: Association Press, 1959.

Coe, George A., *Religious Education Journal*, April 1930, pp. 299, bi-monthly, New York.

——————, *What Is Christian Education?* New York: Charles Scribner's Sons, 1929, pp. 122ff. Out of print.

——————, *World Tomorrow*, June 1932, pp. 175ff. Out of print.

Coffin, Henry Sloane, *The Public Worship of God*. Philadelphia: Westminster Press, 1946.

Elliott, Harrison, *Can Religious Education Be Christian?* New York: Macmillan Company, 1941. Out of print.

Ferre, Nels F. S., *Strengthening the Spiritual Life*. New York: Harper & Row, 1951.

Hardman, Oscar, *A History of Christian Worship*. Nashville: Abingdon Press, 1937.

Hedley, George, *Christian Worship*. New York: Macmillan Co., 1953.

Lee, Florence B. *et al.*, *When Children Worship*. Valley Forge: Judson Press, 1963.

Magee, John, *Reality and Prayer*. New York: Harper & Row, 1957. Unusual.

Maxwell, William D., *An Outline of Christian Worship*. New York: Oxford University Press, 1940.

Shepherd, Massey H., *The Worship of the Church*. New York: Seabury Press, 1952.

Steere, Douglas V., *Time to Spare*. New York: Harper & Row, 1949. For Retreats. Out of print.

Vogt, van Ogden, *Art and Religion*. Boston: Beacon Press, 1960.

——————, *The Primacy of Worship*. Boston: Beacon Press, 1958.

Whiston, Charles F., *Teach Us to Pray*. Philadelphia: United Church Press, 1949.

Williams, J. Paul, *What Americans Believe and How They Worship*. New York: Harper & Row, 1962.

PRAYER

Bro, Margueritte H., *More Than We Are*. New York: Harper & Row, 1948.

Casteel, John L., *Rediscovering Prayer*. New York: Association Press, 1955.

Fosdick, Harry Emerson, *The Meaning of Prayer*. New York: Association Press, 1962.

——————, *A Book of Public Prayers*. New York: Harper & Row, 1959.

Grou, Jean-Nicholas, *How to Pray*. New York: Harper & Row, 1956. Valuable guidance.

Harkness, Georgia, *Prayer and the Common Life*. Nashville: Abingdon Press, 1948.

Law, William, *Serious Call to a Devout and Holy Life*. Naperville: Alec R. Allenson, Inc., 1961.

Lester, Muriel, *Ways of Praying*. Nashville: Abingdon Press, 1940.

Scott, Ernest F., *The Lord's Prayer*, New York: Charles Scribner's Sons, 1951.

Steere, Douglas V., *Dimensions of Prayer*. New York: Harper & Row, 1963.

——————, *Prayer and Worship*. New York: Association Press, 1938.

Straton, Hillyer H., *Prayers in Public*. Valley Forge: Judson Press, 1963.

Temple, William, *The Hope of a New World*. New York: Macmillan Co., 1941. Excellent sections on worship and prayer.

(1) Prayer and the preschool child of 2 to 3

Anderson, Phoebe M., *Religious Living with Nursery Children*. Philadelphia: United Church Press, 1956.

Bannister, Constance and Claxton, Ernest, *A Child's Grace*. New York: E. P. Dutton Co., 1948.

Fritz, Dorothy, *The Spiritual Growth of Children*. Philadelphia: Westminster Press, 1952.

Lee, R. S., *Your Growing Child and Religion*. New York: The Macmillan Co., 1963.

Manwell, Elizabeth, and Fahs, Sophia Lyon, *Consider the Children: How They Grow*. Boston: Beacon Press, 1951.

Strang, Ruth, *A Study of Young Children*. Nashville: Abingdon Press, 1944. Out of print.

(2) Kindergarten (ages 4 and 5)

Jones, Mary Alice, *Tell Me About God*. Chicago: Rand McNally & Co., 1943.

——————, *Prayers and Graces for a Small Child*. Chicago: Rand McNally & Co., 1959.

Lee, R. S., *Your Growing Child and Religion*. New York: Macmillan Co., 1963.

Moore, Jessie E., *Children's Prayers for Everyday*. Nashville: Abingdon Press, 1949.

Wolcott, Carolyn Muller, *God Cares for Me*. Nashville: Abingdon Press, 1958.

(3) Primary (ages 6-8)

Jones, Mary Alice, *God Speaks to Me*. Chicago: Rand McNally & Co., 1961.

——————, *Tell Me About Prayer*. Chicago: Rand McNally & Co., 1948.

Willis, Clarice D. and Stegeman, William H., *Living in the Primary Grades*. Chicago: Follett Publishing Co., 1956.

(4) Junior (ages 9-11)

Bartlett, Robert Merrill, *A Boy's Book of Prayers*. Boston: Pilgrim Press, 1948.

Erb, Bessie P., *In Awe and Wonder*. Philadelphia: United Church Press, 1956.

Jones, Mary Alice, *Tell Me About Prayer*. Chicago: Rand McNally & Co., 1948.

Link, Helen, *Our Father: Thoughts and Prayers for Children*. Philadelphia: United Church Press, 1955.

Sanford, Agnes, *Let's Believe*. New York: Harper & Row, 1954.

Spicer, Dorothy Gladys, *Children's Prayers from Other Lands*. New York: Association Press, 1955.

Taylor, Florence, *Thine Is the Glory*. Philadelphia: Westminster Press, 1949. Interprets Lord's Prayer.

(5) Young People and Adults

Baillie, John, *A Diary of Private Prayers*. New York: Chas. Scribner's Sons, 1949.

Bartlett, Robert Merrill, *With One Voice*. New York: Thomas Y. Crowell Co., 1961. Prayers from around the world.

Bollinger, H. D., *The Student at Prayer*. Nashville: The Upper Room, 1960.

Bro, Margueritte H., *Every Day a Prayer*. New York: Harper & Row, 1943.

Cook, Walter L., *Daily Life Prayers for Youth*. New York: Association Press, 1963. Very useful.

Hayward, Percy R., *Young People's Prayers*. New York: Association Press, 1945.

Herman, Emily, *Creative Prayer*. New York: Harper & Row, 1934.

House, Anne W., *A Girl's Prayer Book*. New York: Seabury Press, 1957.

Johnson, Abigail A., *Prayers for Young People*. Philadelphia: Westminster Press, 1947.

Steere, Douglas V., *On Beginning from Within*. New York: Harper & Row, 1943. Out of print.

Straton, Hillyer H., *Prayers in Public*. Valley Forge: Judson Press, 1963.

Thurman, Howard, *Deep Is the Hunger*. New York: Harper & Row, 1951.

Trueblood, Elton, ed., *Doctor Johnson's Prayers*. New York: Harper & Row, 1947.

——————, *Windows of Worship*. Philadelphia: United Church Press, 1959. A year of devotions for young folks.

SYMBOLISM

Johnson, F. Ernest, *Religious Symbolism*. New York: Harper & Row, 1954. Out of print.

Worship Services and Experiences

(1)   When and how may kindergarten children be led to worship?

Manwell, Elizabeth and Sophia Lyon Fahs, *Consider the Children, How They Grow.* Boston: Beacon Press, 1951.
Maramarco, Phyllis N., *The Kindergarten in the Church.* Hartford: Hartford Seminary Bookstore. Privately published.

(2)   What are effective worship services for primaries and juniors, taking into account such factors as environment, leadership, arrangement of the service, its content, and the experiences around which services are developed?

a.   Primary

Brown, Jeanette P., *As Children Worship.* Philadelphia: United Church Press, 1936.
God-Creator. Greenwich: Seabury Press, 1964. Second grade reader.
Gould, Josephine T., *et al., Teaching Primary Children.* Boston: Beacon Press, 1957.
Jones, J. Orton, *This Is the Way,* New York: Viking Press, 1951.
Wolcott, Carolyn M., *God Planned It That Way.* Nashville: Abingdon Press, 1952.

b.   Junior

Brown, Jeanette P., *Children's Worship in the Church School.* New York: Harper & Row, 1939.
——————, *More Children's Worship in the Church School.* New York: Harper & Row, 1953.
Fitch, Florence, *Book About God.* New York: Lothrop, Lee and Shepard Co., 1953.
Jones, Elizabeth Orton, *Song of the Sun.* New York: Macmillan Co., 1952.
Lee, Florence B., *et al., When Children Worship.* Valley Forge: Judson Press, 1963. (Ages 10-12).
Maramarco, Phyllis N., and Welker, Edith Frances, *As We Think with God.* New York: Abingdon Press, 1962.
Niedermeyer, Mabel A., *When I Think of God,* St. Louis: Bethany Press, 1942. (Ages 6-10).
Poppe, Barbara Peck, *Let's Find Outdoor Opportunities for Worship.* New York: Division of Christian Education, National Council of Churches.

Shields, Elizabeth M., *As the Day Begins*. Richmond: John Knox Press, 1944.

Welker, Edith F., and Barber, Aimee A., *Thoughts of God for Boys and Girls*. New York: Harper & Row, 1948.

(3) Principles to guide in the preparation of worship services (See previous chapters)

Barclay, William, *Epilogues and Prayers*. Nashville: Abingdon Press, 1963.

Bowman, Clarice M., *Worship Ways for Camp*. New York: Association Press, 1955.

Kohn, Harold E., *Reflections*. Grand Rapids: Wm. B. Eerdmans Publishing Co., 1962.

Myers, A. J. William, ed., *Enriching Worship*. New York: Harper & Row, 1949.

Whiston, Charles F., *Teach Us to Pray*. Philadelphia: United Church Press, 1949.

Wickenden, Arthur C., *Concerns of Religion*. New York: Harper & Row, 1959.

(4) Private Resources for Adult Worship

Burkhart, Roy A., *The Person You Can Be*. New York: Harper & Row, 1962. Full of suggestions.

Chase, Mary Ellen, *The Psalms for the Common Reader*. New York: W. W. Norton & Co., Inc., 1962.

Gibran, Kahlil, *Jesus, the Son of Man*. New York: Alfred A. Knopf, 1956. A beautiful book.

Kelly, Thomas, *A Testament of Devotion*. New York: Harper & Row, 1941.

Kepler, Thomas S., ed., *Letters and Reflections of Francois de Fenelon*. Cleveland: World Publishing Co., 1955.

Law, William, ed. by John Meister *et al.*, *A Serious Call to a Devout and Holy Life*. Philadelphia: Westminster Press, 1948.

Lawrence, Brother, *The Practice of the Presence of God*. Naperville: Alec R. Allenson Inc., 1956.

Strong, Mary., ed., *Letters of the Scattered Brotherhood*. New York: Harper & Row, 1948.

Vining, Elizabeth Gray, *The World in Tune*, Wallingford, Pa.: Pendle Hill, 1953.

Wild, John, et al., *Classics of Religious Devotion*. Boston: Beacon Press, 1950.

Family Books

Bedtime Prayers. The Warner Press, Anderson, Indiana. For children. Out of print.

Clough, William A., *Father We Thank Thee.* Nashville: Abingdon Press, 1957.

Fritz, Dorothy B., *The Spiritual Growth of Children.* Philadelphia: Westminster Press, 1957. For parents and teachers.

Gebhart, Anna Laura and Edward W., *Our Family Worships at Home.* Nashville: Abingdon Press, 1958. With children.

LeBar, Mary, *We Learn to Pray.* Cincinnati: Standard Publishing Co., 1963.

Orleans, Ilo, *This Wonderful Day.* New York: Union of American Hebrew Congregations, 1958. Lovely religious poetry.

Seabury Closely Graded Curriculum, Pupils' "take-home books" (one for each grade, kindergarten through fifth). New York: Seabury Press.

Welker, Edith F., and Barber, Aimee A., *Thoughts of God for Boys and Girls.* New York: Harper & Row, 1948.

15.

Scripture in Worship Services

IN THE SIMPLE YET FORMAL SERVICES in which children and young people worship, there are two major uses to be made of biblical materials. The first is the call to worship or to prayer. The second is the material which often *follows* the talk or story and is used either in unison reading or by the leader. Another less frequent use of Scripture is that given by a verse-speaking choir to present some significant event or message. Naturally the loftiest understanding of God in the Bible should influence the leader and guide his thinking.

CALLS TO WORSHIP
FOR CHILDREN'S SERVICES (GRADES TWO TO SIX OR OLDER)

Let the peoples praise thee, O God
It is good to give thanks to the Lord,
to sing praises to thy name . . .
to declare thy steadfast love in the morning . . .
For thou, O Lord, hast made me glad by thy work.
— *Psalm 67:3; 92:1, 2, 4*

O come, let us sing to the Lord . . .
Let us come into his presence with thanksgiving;

167

let us make a joyful noise to him with songs of praise!
For the Lord is a great God . . . .
The sea is his, for he made it . . . .
O come, let us worship . . . . our Maker!
For he is our God.

— Parts of Psalm 95

Know that the Lord is God!
It is he that made us, and we are his;
we are his people . . . .
Give thanks to him . . . .
For the Lord is good;
his steadfast love endures forever.

— Parts of Psalm 100

It is good to give thanks to the Lord . . . .
Thank the Lord for his steadfast love,
for his wonderful works to the sons of men! . . .
O give thanks to the Lord, for he is good;
his steadfast love endures forever!

— Psalm 92:1; 107:31; 118:1

Thou are my God, and I will give thanks to thee;
thou art my God, I will extol thee.
O give thanks to the Lord, for he is good;
his steadfast love endures forever!

— Psalm 118:28, 29

CALLS TO WORSHIP

FOR GRADES SEVEN AND UPWARDS

Serve the Lord with gladness
Come into his presence with singing!
Know that the Lord is God!
It is he that made us, and we are his;
we are his people.

— Psalm 100:2, 3

Enter his gates with thanksgiving,
    and his courts with praise!
Give thanks to him, bless his name!
For the Lord is good;
    his steadfast love endures forever,
    and his faithfulness to all generations.

— Psalm 100:4, 5

O give thanks to the Lord, for he is good;
for his steadfast love endures forever! . . .
Let them thank the Lord for his steadfast love,
for his wonderful works to the sons of men!
Let them extol him in the congregation of the people.

— Psalm 107:1, 31, 32

Bless the Lord, O my soul!
O Lord my God, thou art very great!
Thou art clothed with honor and majesty . . . .
O Lord, how manifold are thy works!
In wisdom hast thou made them all;
    the earth is full of thy creatures . . . .
I will sing to the Lord as long as I live;
I will sing praise to my God while I have being.

— Psalm 104:1, 24, 33

O give thanks to the Lord, call on his name,
make known his deeds among the peoples!
Sing to him, sing praises to him,
tell of all his wonderful works! . . .
Seek the Lord and his strength,
    seek his presence continually!
Remember the wonderful works that he has done.

— Psalm 105:1, 2, 4, 5a

For thou, O Lord, art good and forgiving,
    abounding in steadfast love to all who call on thee . . . .
For thou art great and doest wondrous things,
    thou alone art God.
Teach me thy way, O Lord, that I may walk in thy truth;
    unite my heart to fear thy name.

— Psalm 86:5, 10, 11

O give thanks to the Lord, for he is good,
    for his steadfast love endures forever.
O give thanks to the God of gods,
    for his steadfast love endures forever.
O give thanks to the Lord of lords,
    for his steadfast love endures forever;
to him who alone does great wonders,
    for his steadfast love endures forever.

— Psalm 136:1-4

It is good to give thanks to the Lord,
   to sing praises to thy name, O Most High;
to declare thy steadfast love in the morning,
   and thy faithfulness by night . . . .
For thou, O Lord, hast made me glad by thy work;
   at the works of thy hands I sing for joy.
How great are thy works, O Lord!
   Thy thoughts are very deep!

                                    — *Psalm 92:1, 2, 4, 5*

Other recommended selections are: Psalm 106:1, 47; Psalm 122:1; Psalm 146:1, 2; Psalm 147:1, 7; Psalm 148:1, 3, 4, 5, 6, 13.

SCRIPTURE AFTER THE CONCRETENESS IN THE CHILDREN'S SERVICE OF WORSHIP (AGES SEVEN THROUGH ELEVEN OR OLDER)

It is effective to use Scripture to summarize the main emphasis, after a story or a talk in a worship service for children and young people. Usually this same Scripture is used during the entire period covered by a single theme, perhaps five or six weeks. It is helpful if the whole worshiping group memorizes this in advance. Otherwise, it may be read in unison from a chart or a prepared service.

Let the words of my mouth and the meditation of my heart
   be acceptable in thy sight,
O Lord . . . .

                                    — *Psalm 19:14*

Make me to know thy ways, O Lord;
   teach me thy paths.
Lead me in thy truth, and teach me.

                                    — *Psalm 25:4, 5*

O Lord my God, thou art very great!
Thou art clothed with honor and majesty . . . .
I will sing to the Lord as long as I live;
   I will sing praise to my God.

                                    — *Psalm 104:1, 33*

Stop and consider the wondrous works of God . . . .

— Job 37:14

The heavens are telling the glory of God;
and the firmament proclaims his handiwork.

— Job 37:14, Psalm 19:1

O Lord, our Lord,
how majestic is thy name in all the earth! . . .
When I look at thy heavens . . .
the moon and the stars which thou hast established;
what is man that thou art mindful of him . . . ?
Yet thou hast made him little less than God . . . .
Thou hast given him dominion over the works of thy hands . . . .
O Lord, our Lord,
how majestic is thy name in all the earth!

— Psalm 8:1, 3, 5, 6, 9

The earth is the Lord's . . .
the world and those who dwell therein.

— Psalm 24:1

You have heard that it was said, "You shall love your neighbor and
hate your enemy." But I say to you, Love your enemies and pray
for those who persecute you, so that you may be sons of your Father
who is in heaven; for he makes his sun rise on the evil and on the
good, and sends rain on the just and on the unjust. For if you
love those who love you, what reward have you? Do not even the
tax collectors do the same? And if you salute only your brethren,
what more are you doing than others? Do not even the Gentiles
do the same? You, therefore, must be perfect, as your heavenly
Father is perfect.

— Matthew 5:43-48

Blessed is he who considers the poor . . . .
Do not withhold good from those to whom it is due,
when it is in your power to do it.
Do not say to your neighbor, "Go, and come again,
tomorrow I will give it" — when you have it with you.

— Psalm 41:1, Proverbs 3:27, 28

And a poor widow came, and put in two copper coins, which make a penny. And he called his disciples to him, and said to them, "Truly, I say to you, this poor widow has put in more than all those who are contributing to the treasury. For they all contributed out of their abundance; but she out of her poverty has put in everything she had, her whole living."

— Mark 12:42-44

Finally, all of you, have unity of spirit, sympathy, love of the brethren, a tender heart and a humble mind. Do not return evil for evil . . . .

Love your enemies, do good to those who hate you . . . .

See what love the Father has given us, that we should be called children of God; and so we are. . . . For this is the message which you have heard from the beginning, that we should love one another.

—I Peter 3:8, 9; Luke 6:27; I John 3:1, 11

And he made from one every nation of men to live on all the face of the earth . . . . For love is of God, and he who loves is born of God and knows God.

— Acts 17:26; I John 4:7

Love is patient and kind; love is not jealous or boastful; it is not arrogant or rude. Love does not insist on its own way; it is not irritable or resentful; it does not rejoice at wrong, but rejoices in the right. Love bears all things, believes all things, hopes all things, endures all things.

Love never ends; as for prophecy, it will pass away; as for tongues, they will cease; as for knowledge, it will pass away.

— I Corinthians 13:4-8

No man has ever seen God; if we love one another, God abides in us and his love is perfected in us . . . . God is love . . . . God is spirit . . . . You are God's temple and . . . God's spirit dwells in you.

— I John 4:12, 16; John 4:24; I Corinthians 3:16

Scripture for Youth (Age Twelve and Upwards)

GOD AS CREATOR

Thus says God, the Lord,
   who created the heavens . . .

who spread forth the earth and what comes from it,
who gives breath to the people upon it
    and spirit to those who walk in it:
"I am the Lord, I have called you in righteousness."

— Isaiah 42:5, 6

The heavens are telling the glory of God;
    and the firmament proclaims his handiwork.

— Psalm 19:1

Thine is the day, thine also the night;
    thou hast established the luminaries and the sun.

— Psalm 74:16

The heavens are thine, the earth also is thine;
    the world and all that is in it, thou hast founded them.

— Psalm 89:11

Before the mountains were brought forth,
    or ever thou hadst formed the earth and the world,
    from everlasting to everlasting thou art God.

— Psalm 90:2

O come, let us worship and bow down,
    let us kneel before the Lord, our Maker!
For he is our God,
    and we are the people of his pasture,
    and the sheep of his hand.
O that today you would hearken to his voice!

— Psalm 95:6, 7

Know that the Lord is God!
    It is he that made us, and we are his;
    we are his people.

— Psalm 100:3

Happy is he whose . . . hope is in the Lord his God,
who made heaven and earth,
    the sea, and all that is in them;
who keeps faith forever;
    who executes justice for the oppressed;
    who gives food to the hungry.

— Psalm 146:5-7

GOD IS GOOD

For the Lord is righteous, he loves righteous deeds.

— Psalm 11:7

Good and upright is the Lord;
    therefore he instructs sinners in the way.
He leads the humble in what is right,
    and teaches the humble his way.
All the paths of the Lord are steadfast love and faithfulness,
    for those who keep his covenant and his testimonies.

— Psalm 25:8-10

For thou, O Lord, are good and forgiving,
    abounding in steadfast love to all who call on thee.

— Psalm 86:5

SUSTAINER OF LIFE

Thou makest springs gush forth in the valleys;
    they flow between the hills,
they give drink to every beast of the field . . . .
by them the birds of the air have their habitation;
    they sing among the branches.
From thy lofty abode thou waterest the mountains;
    the earth is satisfied with the fruit of thy work.
Thou dost cause the grass to grow for the cattle,
    and plants for man to cultivate,
that he may bring forth food from the earth.

— Psalm 104:10-14

Have you not known? Have you not heard?
The Lord is the everlasting God,
    the Creator of the ends of the earth.
He does not faint or grow weary,
    his understanding is unsearchable.

— Isaiah 40:28

Remember to extol his work,
    of which men have sung.
All men have looked on it;
    man beholds it from afar.
Behold, God is great, and we know him not;
    the number of his years is unsearchable.

For he draws up the drops of water,
  he distils his mist in rain
which the skies pour down,
  and drop upon man abundantly.
Can any one understand the spreading of the clouds,
  the thunderings of his pavilion?
Behold, he scatters his lightning about him,
  and covers the roots of the sea.

— Job 36:24-30

He determines the number of the stars,
  he gives to all of them their names.
Great is our Lord, and abundant in power;
  his understanding is beyond measure . . . .
He covers the heavens with clouds,
  he prepares rain for the earth,
  he makes grass grow upon the hills.

— Psalm 147:4, 5, 8

He sends forth his command to the earth;
  his word runs swiftly.
He gives snow like wool;
  he scatters hoarfrost like ashes.
He casts forth his ice like morsels;
  who can stand before his cold?

— Psalm 147:15-17

PLACE OF MAN

When I look at thy heavens, the work of thy fingers,
  the moon and the stars which thou hast established;
what is man that thou art mindful of him,
  and the son of man that thou dost care for him?
Yet thou hast made him little less than God,
  and dost crown him with glory and honor.
Thou hast given him dominion over the works of thy hands;
  thou hast put all things under his feet,
all sheep and oxen,
  and also the beasts of the field,
the birds of the air, and the fish of the sea,
  whatever passes along the paths of the sea.
O Lord, our Lord,
  how majestic is thy name in all the earth!

— Psalm 8:3-9

PLACE OF GOD

I am the Lord, and there is no other,
    besides me there is no God . . . .
Turn to me and be saved, all the ends of the earth!
    For I am God, and there is no other.

— *Isaiah 45:5, 22*

Seek the Lord while he may be found,
    call upon him while he is near;
let the wicked forsake his way,
    and the unrighteous man his thoughts;
let him return to the Lord, that he may have mercy on him,
    and to our God, for he will abundantly pardon.
For my thoughts are not your thoughts,
    neither are your ways my ways, says the Lord.
For as the heavens are higher than the earth,
    so are my ways higher than your ways
    and my thoughts than your thoughts.

— *Isaiah 55:6-9*

For all who are led by the Spirit of God are sons of God.

— *Romans 8:14*

He who searches the hearts of men knows what is in the mind of
the Spirit.

— *Romans 8:27*

We know that in everything God works for good with those who
love him, who are called according to his purpose.

— *Romans 8:28*

If God is for us, who is against us?

— *Romans 8:31*

For I am sure that neither death, nor life, nor angels, nor princi-
palities, nor things present, nor things to come, nor powers, nor
height, nor depth, nor anything else in all creation, will be able
to separate us from the love of God.

— *Romans 8:38, 39*

There is no distinction between Jew and Greek; the same Lord is
Lord of all.   *Romans 10:12*

Do you not know that you are God's temple, and that God's
Spirit dwells within you? . . . God's temple is holy, and that
temple you are.

— *1 Corinthians 3:16, 17*

LIVING AS CHILDREN OF GOD

I appeal to you therefore, brethren, by the mercies of God, to
present your bodies as a living sacrifice, holy and acceptable to
God . . . . Do not be conformed to this world but be transformed
by the renewal of your mind, that you may prove what is the will
of God, what is good and acceptable and perfect . . . . Let love be
genuine; hate what is evil, hold fast to what is good; love one
another with brotherly affection.

— *Romans 12:1, 2, 9, 10*

Live in harmony with one another; do not be haughty, but associate with the lowly; never be conceited. Repay no one evil for
evil . . . live peaceably with all. . . . Never avenge yourselves.
. . . If your enemy is hungry, feed him; if he is thirsty, give him
drink; for by so doing you will heap burning coals upon his head.
Do not be overcome by evil, but overcome evil with good.

— *Parts of Romans 12:16-21*

None of us lives to himself, and none of us dies to himself. If we
live, we live to the Lord, and if we die, we die to the Lord; so
then, whether we live or whether we die, we are the Lord's.

— *Romans 14:7, 8*

I desire mercy, and not sacrifice.   —*Matthew 9:13a*

He has showed you, O man, what is good;
    and what does the Lord require of you
but to do justice, and to love kindness,
    and to walk humbly with your God?

— *Micah 6:8*

Let no one seek his own good, but the good of his neighbor.

— *1 Corinthians 10:24*

You shall love your neighbor as yourself.

— *Galatians 5:14*

The fruit of the Spirit is love, joy, peace, patience, kindness, goodness, faithfulness, gentleness, self-control.

— Galatians 5:22, 23

Whatever is true, whatever is honorable, whatever is just, whatever is pure, whatever is lovely, whatever is gracious, if there is any excellence, if there is anything worthy of praise, think about these things.

— Philippians 4:8

You shall not hate your brother in your heart, but you shall reason with your neighbor, lest you bear sin because of him. You shall not take vengeance or bear any grudge against the sons of your own people, but you shall love your neighbor as yourself. I am the Lord.

— Leviticus 19:17, 18

16.
Worship Stories and Talks

The Sky

Schneider, Herman and Nina, *You Among the Stars*. New York: W. R. Scott, 1951.

Stevens, Bertha, *How Miracles Abound*. Boston: Beacon Press, 1941.

Zim, Herbert S., *The Sun*. New York: Wm. Morrow & Co., 1953.

The World Around Us

Ames, Gerald, and Rose Wyler, *The First Days of the World*. New York: Harper & Row, 1958. Story of earliest beginnings.

Bell, Thelma, *Snow*. New York: Viking Press, 1954.

Blough, Glenn O., *Not Only for Ducks*. New York: McGraw-Hill Book Co., 1954.

Buck, Margaret W., *In Ponds and Streams*. Nashville: Abingdon Press, 1955.

Buck, Pearl, *The Big Wave*. New York: John Day Co., 1948.

God-Creator (second grade). Greenwich: Seabury Press, 1964.

Hader, Berta and Elmer, *The Big Snow*. New York: Macmillan Co., 1948.

Marcher, Marion, *Monarch Butterfly*. New York: Holiday House, 1954.

Stefferude, Alfred, *The Wonder of Seeds*. New York: Harcourt, Brace & World, 1956.

Williams, Henry L., *Stories in Rocks*. New York: Holt, Rinehart & Winston, 1948.

Christmas

Cavanah, Frances, comp., *Favorite Christmas Stories*. New York: Grosset & Dunlap, Inc., 1949. Formerly published as *Told Under the Christmas Tree*.

Kunhardt, Dorothy, *Once There Was a Little Boy*. New York: Viking Press, 1946.

Luckhardt, Mildred, *The Story of St. Nicholas*. Nashville: Abingdon Press, 1960.

People Who Represent Important Aspects of Living

Alofsin, Dorothy, *America's Triumph*. Union of American Hebrew Congregations, 1956. Ten great founders of America.

Bontemps, Arna, *Frederick Douglass: Slave, Fighter, Freeman*. New York: Alfred P. Knopf, 1959.

Dalgliesh, Alice, *The Courage of Sarah Noble*. New York: Charles Scribner's Sons, 1954.

Dooley, Thomas A., *The Edge of Tomorrow*. New York: Farrar, Straus & Co., 1958.

Eaton, Jeanette, *Lone Journey*. New York: Harcourt, Brace & Co. Inc., 1944.

——————, *Gandhi, Fighter Without a Sword*. New York: Wm. Morrow & Co., 1950.

Fisher, Dorothy Canfield, *And Long Remember*. New York: McGraw-Hill Book Co., 1959. Stories of some great Americans.

Freeman, Mae B., *The Story of Albert Einstein*. New York: Random House, 1958.

Gilbert, Miriam, *Jane Addams*. Nashville: Abingdon Press, 1960.

Gollomb, Joseph, *Albert Schweitzer*. New York: Vanguard Press, 1949.

Graham, Shirley, *The Story of Phyllis Wheatley*. New York: Julian Messner, 1949.

Gray, Elizabeth Janet, *Penn*. New York: Viking Press, 1938.

Hagedorn, Hermann, *Prophet in the Wilderness*. New York: Macmillan Co., 1954.

Holt, Rackham, *George Washington Carver*. Garden City: Doubleday & Co., 1942.

Hughes, Langston, *Famous American Negroes*. New York: Dodd, Mead & Co., 1954.

——————, *Famous Negro Heroes of America*. New York: Dodd, Mead & Co., 1958.

Hunter, Allan A., *Courage in Both Hands*. New York: Ballantine Books, Inc., 1962.

Kenworthy, Leonard S., *Twelve Citizens of the World*. Garden City: Doubleday & Co., 1953.

King, Jr., Martin Luther, *Stride Toward Freedom*. New York: Harper & Row, 1958.

Kugelmass, J. Alvin, *Ralph J. Bunche*. New York: Julian Messner, 1962.

Levinger, Elma, *Albert Einstein*. New York: Julian Messner, Inc., 1949.

Masani, Shakuntala, *Nehru's Story*. Oxford University Press, 1949.

Mason, Cora, *Socrates: The Man Who Dared To Ask*. Boston: Beacon Press, 1953. Excellent for young people.

McNeer, May Y., *Martin Luther*. Nashville: Abingdon Press, 1953.

McNeer, May Y. and Ward, Lynd K., *Armed with Courage*. Nashville: Abingdon Press, 1957. Stories of Florence Nightingale, Father Damien, George Washington Carver, Jane Addams, Wilfred Grenfell, Mahatma Gandhi, and Albert Schweitzer.

Pearle, Catherine Owens, *The Helen Keller Story*. New York: Thomas Y. Crowell Co., 1959.

Simon, Charlie May, *A Seed Shall Serve*. The story of Toyohiko Kagawa. New York: E. P. Dutton & Co., 1959.

Sterne, Emma Gelders, *Mary McLeod Bethune*. New York: Alfred P. Knopf, 1957.

Turnbull, E. Lucia, *The Legends of the Saints*. Philadelphia: J. B. Lippincott Co., 1959.

Vorspan, Albert, *Giants of Justice*. New York: Union of American Hebrew Congregations, 1960.

Williams, Beryl, *Lillian Wald*. New York: Julian Messner, 1948.

Wilson, Dorothy C., *Dr. Ida*. New York: McGraw-Hill Book Co., 1959.

Workers

Baxter, Edna M., *Living and Working in Our Country*. Nashville: Abingdon Press, 1938.

Lenski, Lois, *Judy's Journey*. New York: Oxford University Press, 1955.

——————, *Cotton in My Sack*. Philadelphia: J. B. Lippincott Co., 1949.

God and His World

Andrews, Dorothy W., *God's World and Johnny* (first grade). Philadelphia: Westminster Press, 1948.

Fitch, Florence M., *A Book About God* (primary age). New York: Lothrop, Lee & Shepard Co., 1953.

God-Creator (second grade reader). Greenwich: Seabury Press, 1964.

Jones, Mary Alice, *God Is Good*. Chicago: Rand McNally & Co., 1956.

Pilkington, Roger, *In the Beginning* (for adult leaders). New York: St. Martin's Press, 1957.

Watson, Jane W., *My Golden Book About God*. New York: Golden Press, 1957.

Friendship Towards Many People

Beim, Jerrold, *The Smallest Boy in the Class*. New York: Wm. Morrow & Co., 1949.

Bishop, Claire H., *All Alone*. New York: Viking Press, 1952.

Bowles, Cynthia, *At Home in India*. New York: Harcourt, Brace & World, 1956.

Faulkner, Georgene, *Melindy's Happy Summer*. New York: Julian Messner, 1949.

Knight, Ruth Adams, *It Might Be You*. Garden City: Doubleday & Co., 1949.

Krauss, Ruth, *The Big World and the Little House*. New York: Harper & Row, 1956.

Rosenheim, Lucile G., *Kathie, the New Teacher*. New York: Julian Messner, 1949.

(Also write Anti-Defamation League, 315 Lexington Avenue, New York, for children's stories.)

Refugees and War's Peoples

Bishop, Claire H., *Twenty and Ten*. New York: Viking Press, 1952. For juniors.

Hunt, Mabel L., *Singing Among Strangers*. Philadelphia: J. B. Lippincott Co., 1954.

Kim, Yong, *The Happy Days*. Boston: Little, Brown & Co., 1960.

Seymour, Alta H., *Toward Morning*. Chicago: Follett Publishing Co., 1961. Hungarian Youth Freedom Fighters.

Story Collections

Allstrom, Elizabeth, *Round Window*. New York: Friendship Press, 1953.

Angle, Paul M., ed., *Lincoln Reader*. New York: Affiliated Publishers, 1947.

Applegarth, Margaret T., *Right Here, Right Now*. New York: Harper & Row, 1950.

Arbuthnot, May Hill, *Arbuthnot Anthology*. New York: W. R. Scott Inc., 1961.

Broomell, Anna P., *The Friendly Story Caravan*. Philadelphia: J. B. Lippincott Co., 1949.

Brown, Jeannette P., *Storyteller in Religious Education*. Boston: Pilgrim Press, 1951.

Caffrey, N., *Penny's Worth*. New York: E. P. Dutton & Co., 1952.

Cathon, Laura E., and Thusnelda Schmidt, *Treasured Tales*. Nashville: Abingdon Press, 1960.

Evans, Eva Knox, *People Are Important* (chapter on fighting). New York: Capitol Publishing, 1951.

Fahs, Sophia L., *From Long Ago and Many Lands*. Boston: Beacon Press, 1948.

Forster, E. M., *Two Cheers for Democracy*. New York: Harcourt, Brace & World, 1962.

Gruenberg, Sidonie M., *Favorite Stories Old and New*. Garden City: Doubleday & Co., 1955.

Hazeltine, Alice I., *Children's Stories to Read and Tell*. Nashville: Abingdon Press, 1949.

——————, *Easter Book of Legends and Stories*. New York: Lothrop, Lee & Shepard, 1947.

——————, *Selected Stories for Teen-agers*. Nashville: Abingdon Press, 1952.

Holiday Storybook. Child Study Association of America. New York: Thomas Y. Crowell Co., 1952.

Kelsey, Alice G., *Stories for Junior Worship*. Nashville: Abingdon Press, 1941.

——————, *Teakwood Pulpit and Other Stories for Junior Worship*. Nashville: Abingdon Press, 1950.

Kenworthy, Leonard, *Twelve Citizens of the World*. Garden City: Doubleday & Co., 1954.

Knight, Ruth Adams, *It Might Be You*. Garden City: Doubleday & Co., 1949.

Kunhardt, Dorothy, *Once There Was a Little Boy*. New York: Viking Press, 1946.

Millen, Nina, *Missionary Story Hour*. New York: Friendship Press, 1952.

Niebuhr, Hulda, *Greatness Passing By*. New York: Charles Scribner's Sons, 1931.

Odell, Mary C., *Story Shop*. Valley Forge: Judson Press, 1951.

Pannell, Lucile, and Frances Cavanah, *Holiday Round-Up*. Philadelphia: Macrae Smith Co., 1950.

Russell, Ruth W., *Stories You Can Tell*. Valley Forge: Judson Press, 1963.

Saint-Exupery, Antoine de, *Wind, Sand, and Stars*. New York: Harcourt, Brace & World, Inc., 1954.

Schneider, Herman and Nina, *Follow the Sunset*. Garden City: Doubleday & Co., 1952.

Smith, Lillian, *Killers of the Dream,* New York: Norton & Co., 1961.

Steinbeck, John, *The Red Pony*. New York: Viking Press, 1959.

Watson, Katherine W., ed., *Tales for Telling*. New York: H. W. Wilson Co., 1950.

Wilder, Laura I., *The Little House in the Big Woods* (One of a Series). New York: Harper & Row, 1953.

Single Stories

Buck, Pearl, *The Big Wave*. New York: John Day Co., 1948.

Caffrey, Nancy, *Penny's Worth*. New York: E. P. Dutton Co., 1952.

Knight, Ruth Adams, *It Might Be You*. Garden City: Doubleday & Co.

Saint-Exupery, Antoine de, *Wind, Sand, and Stars*. New York: Harcourt, Brace & World, Inc., 1954. Story of Guillamet and a crash landing.

Schneider, Herman and Nina, *Follow the Sunset*. Garden City: Doubleday & Co., 1952.

Smith, Lillian, *The Journey* (Ch. 12, a mother in relation to tragedy; Ch. 10, the power of a teacher). Cleveland: World Publishing Co., 1954.

Wilder, Laura I., *The Little House in the Big Woods* (one of a series). New York: Harper & Row, 1953.

Wolfe, Louis, *Independence of Tabitha Brown* (a pioneer woman going to Salem, Oregon), *Reader's Digest*, August 1954, p 73.

Stories and Resources for Young People at Worship

Baxter, Edna M., *Living and Working in Our Country*. Nashville: Abingdon Press, 1938.

Fitzgerald, Lawrence P., *Adventures in Christian Living*. Valley Forge: Judson Press, 1964.

Graham, Alberta P., *Clara Barton*. Nashville: Abingdon Press, 1956.

Milner-White, Eric, and G. W. Briggs, eds., *Daily Prayer*. New York: Oxford University Press, 1941.

Myers, A. J. William, ed., *Enriching Worship*. New York: Harper & Row, 1949.

Niebuhr, Hulda, *Greatness Passing By*. New York: Charles Scribner's Sons, 1931.

Silliman, Vincent, *We Speak of Life*. Boston: Beacon Press, 1955.

Thurman, Howard, *Deep Is the Hunger*. New York: Harper & Row, 1951.

Drama in Worship

Alexander, Ryllis C. and Goslin, O. P., *Worship Through Drama*. New York: Harper & Row, 1930.

Eastman, Fred, *Modern Religious Drama*. New York: Harper & Row, 1938.

Ehrensperger, Harold, *Religious Drama, Ends and Means*. Nashville: Abingdon Press, 1962.

Eliot, T. S., *Murder in the Cathedral*. New York: Harcourt, Brace & World, Inc., 1938.

Johnson, Albert, *Drama: Technique and Philosophy*. Valley Forge: Judson Press, 1963.

POETRY IN WORSHIP

Beacon Song and Service Book. Boston: Beacon Press, 1960.

Burkhart, Roy A., *et al, At Worship: A Hymnal for Young Churchmen*. New York: Harper & Row, 1951.

Clark, Thomas Curtis and Gillespie, Esther A., *One Thousand Quotable Poems*. Chicago: Willett, Clark and Co., 1937.

Eliot, T. S., *Four Quartets*. New York: Harcourt, Brace & World, Inc., 1954.

Leavens, Robert F., *Good Companions* (Anthology of prose and verse gathered from all recorded time—good.) Boston: Beacon Press, 1941.

Morrison, James Dalton, ed., *Masterpieces of Religions Verse*. New York: Harper & Row, 1948.

Seager, Ralph, *Christmas Chimes in Rhyme*. Valley Forge: Judson Press, 1962.

17.
Music for All Ages at Worship

Books

Nursery and Kindergarten Resources

Coleman, Satis N., *Another Dancing Time*. New York: John Day Co., 1962.

Coleman, Satis N. and Thorn, Alice G., *Little Singing Time*. New York: John Day Co., 1940.

————, *Singing Time*. New York: John Day Co., 1929.

————, *Another Singing Time*. New York: John Day Co., 1937.

————, *Singing Time Growing Up*. New York: John Day Co., 1958.

Diller, Angela and Page, *Pre-School Music Book* (rhythms). New York: G. Schirmer Inc., n. d.

Sheehy, Emma D., *Children Discover Music & Dance*. New York: Holt, Rinehart & Winston, 1959.

Thomas, Edith Lovell, *Martin and Judy Songs*. Boston: Beacon Press, 1959.

Songs for Early Childhood in Church and Home. Philadelphia: Westminster Press, 1958.

Primary Resources

Brown, Jeanette P., *As Children Worship*. Philadelphia: United Church, 1936.

————, *Children's Worship in the Church School.* New York: Harper & Row, 1939.

Beacon Song and Service Book. Boston: Beacon Press, 1960.

Landeck, Beatrice, *Songs to Grow On.* New York: Wm. Morrow & Co., 1950. Good for ages 4-9.

Seeger, Ruth Crawford, *American Folk Songs for Children.* Garden City: Doubleday & Co., 1948.

Thomas, Edith L., *Sing, Children, Sing.* Nashville: Abingdon Press, 1939.

Junior Resources

Beacon Song and Service Book. Boston: Beacon Press, 1960.

Hymns for Junior Worship. Philadelphia: Westminster Press, 1940.

Pilgrim Hymnal. Boston: Pilgrim Press, 1958. Many excellent resources for all occasions.

Thomas, Edith Lovell, ed., *Singing Worship with Boys and Girls.* Nashville: Abingdon Press, 1958.

Resources for Young People and Adults

There are many excellent hymnals available. This author is partial to *At Worship: A Hymnal for Young Churchmen* (New York: Harper & Row, 1951), *Beacon Song and Service Book* (Boston: Beacon Press, 1960), and *Pilgrim Hymnal* (Boston: Pilgrim Press, 1958). The *Pilgrim Hymnal,* created for general use, is a rich resource for all ages, containing beautiful and noble music from many traditions, countries, and cultures. The following are other helpful books:

Bailey, Albert E., *The Gospel in Hymns.* New York: Charles Scribner's Sons, 1951.

Clokey, Joseph W., *In Every Corner Sing.* New York: Morehouse-Barlow Co., 1945.

Coleman, Satis N. and Jorgensen, E. K., *Christmas Carols from Many Lands.* New York: G. Schirmer Inc., 1934. A superb collection.

Davison, Archibald T., *Protestant Church Music in America.* Boston: E. C. Schirmer Co., 1933.

Dickinson, Edward, *Music in the History of the Western Church.* New York: Charles Scribner's Sons, 1902.

Ellinwood, Leonard W., *The History of American Church Music.* New York: Morehouse-Gorham Co., 1953.

Mursell, James L., *Education for Musical Growth.* Boston: Ginn & Co., 1948.

Silliman, Vincent, ed., *We Sing of Life*. Boston: Beacon Press, 1955.

Thomas, Edith Lovell, *The Whole World Singing*. New York: Friendship Press, 1958.

SELECTED HYMNS AND SONGS

Nursery and Kindergarten

JOY AND PRAISE

Sing a Song of a Rainy Day	In the Woods
Now We Sing a Song	Moon and Sun
Spring Song	Can Anyone Know?

SOCIAL RELATIONSHIPS

The Postman	Friends
The Farmer	The Doctor
Vegetable Man	Everybody
Home	

EASTER

Spring Song	Easter Time
In the Woods	Robin in the Rain
Spring Time	

CHRISTMAS

Christmas Bells	Christmas Song
Carol Children	

Primary

JOY AND PEACE

A World to Know	The Winter Air Is Crisp and Cold
How Wonderful!	All the Happy Children
Healing, Strength and Joy	Wonderings
Loaf of Bread	Sure Is the Sun
A Seed Song	

JESUS

Doing Friendly Things	Boy of Palestine

SOCIAL RELATIONSHIPS

Workmen We Never See	Great Round Sun
Friends of All	It Is Very Good to Be
The Many, Many Children	

INTROITS AND RESPONSES

If With All Your Hearts
Lord, Who Lovest Little
   Children

Hear Us, Our Father
I Will Sing
Come with Hearts Rejoicing

EASTER

The Earth Awakes from
   Winter Sleep
Praise Be to God!
Lo, the Winter Is Past

Blue Sky, Soft and Clear
   (very high: play and sing
   in a lower key)
Joy Is Abroad

CHRISTMAS

Kolyada

Play Sweet Music

Junior

JESUS

(Hymns marked with * are also graded for Junior-high Worship.)

At Work Beside His Father's
   Bench
Far Away in Old Judea

*O Master Workman of the
   Race

GOD-WORSHIP

This Is My Father's World
God Speaks to Us

*Best of All the Things We Do
   (dedication)

PRAISE

Praise to the Lord (possible
   junior choir selection)
We Thy People Praise Thee
   (junior choir has variation in
   tune and ideas)
For Man's Unceasing Quest
   for God (sweep of religion)

*O God, Whose Love Is Over
   All (highly recommended)
*O God, Our Help in Ages Past
*The God of Abraham Praise
All That's Good and Great and
   True (tune: Orientis Partibus)
Ever Faithful, Ever Sure

RESPONSES

*The Lord Is in His Holy
   Temple
Holy, Holy, Holy
*Praise Ye the Lord (Psalm 150)
O Come, Let Us Worship
   (call to worship)

Thy Work, O God, Needs Many
   Hands (offering, first stanza
   only)
*We Give Thee but Thine
   Own (offering)
Seek Ye the Lord

PRAYER

Hear Us Our Father
I Thank You, God

Father, Hear the Prayer We
   Offer

CHURCH

His Own Church (Jesus)
Our Church (Praise)

*Forward Through the Ages

SPECIAL OCCASIONS

Christmas Bells
Spring Has Now Unwrapped
the Flowers
Christ Triumphant (Easter)

The Glory of the Spring (Easter)
*O Come, O Come, Emmanuel
(Christmas)

WORKERS

*Now Praise We Great and
Famous Men
O Son of Man (Jesus as a
worker)

Workers Together
We Plow the Fields
*All the World's Working
The Workers

RACE AND NATION, WORLD FRIENDSHIP, SOCIAL

*Where Cross the Crowded Ways
(sixth grade and above)
My Country is the World
All the World

The World One Neighborhood
God Loves His Children
Everywhere
The Brotherhood of Man

GOD IN HIS WORLD

*The Heavens Declare Thy
Glory (strong hymn)
*God of the Earth, the Sky, the
Sea (Use with older juniors,
junior high)
For the Beauty of the Earth

O Painter of the Fruits and
Flowers
*Maker of the Planets
Autumn Praise
In Summer Fields
*God's Plan

Youth and Adults

PRAISE AND WORSHIP

Holy, Holy, Holy
The God of Abraham Praise
Now Thank We All Our God
My God, I Thank Thee Who Hast
Made (Tune: *Wentworth*)
Joyful, Joyful, We Adore Thee
From All That Dwell Below the
Skies
For the Beauty of the Earth
The Day Thou Gavest

Eternal Ruler of the Ceaseless
Round
O God, Whose Love Is Over All
All Creatures of Our God and
King
We Praise Thee, O God
We Gather Together
All People that on Earth Do
Dwell
Worship the Lord in the Beauty
of Holiness

Praise to the Lord, the Almighty (v. 1, 3)
Let Us With a Gladsome Mind
Rejoice, Ye Pure in Heart
Father, Give Thy Benediction
O God, Our Help in Ages Past
God of the Earth, the Sky, the Sea
God of Our Fathers, Whose Almighty Hand
Now Praise We Great and Famous Men
Eternal, Unchanging, We Sing to Thy Praise

JESUS

O Master Workman of the Race
O Young and Fearless Prophet
Strong Son of God, Immortal Love
Now in the Days of Youth
Where Cross the Crowded Ways of Life
O Come, O Come, Emmanuel
Once to Every Man and Nation
(See *Christmas* and *Easter*)

THE CHURCH

Faith of Our Fathers
God of Grace and God of Glory
Rise Up, O Men of God
Once to Every Man and Nation
O Where Are Kings and Empires Now
God Send Us Men . . .

GOD'S CREATIVE POWER IN NATURE

For the Beauty of the Earth
Day Is Dying in the West
All Creatures of Our God and King
The Spacious Firmament on High
This Is My Father's World
O Beautiful for Spacious Skies
God of the Earth, the Sky, the Sea
For Flowers that Bloom about Our Feet
Seek Not Afar for Beauty . . .
All Beautiful the March of Days
We Plow the Fields
O Life, That Makest All Things New
My God, I Thank Thee
All Nature's Works His Praise Declare

SOCIAL RELATIONSHIPS

Once to Every Man and Nation
O Young and Fearless Prophet
Rise Up, O Men of God
God of Grace, and God of Glory
Be Strong, We Are Not Here to Play . . .
Where Cross the Crowded Ways of Life
All People that on Earth do Dwell
The Voice of God Is Calling
We Thank Thee, Lord, thy Paths of Service Lead
That Cause Can Neither Be Lost Nor Stayed

O Brother Man, Fold to Thy
Heart Thy Brother (omit v. 2)
In Christ There Is No East or
West

Turn Back, O Man, Forswear
Thy Foolish Ways
Eternal God, Whose Power
Upholds

THE NEW YEAR

Ring Out, Wild Bells, to the
Wild Sky
God Send Us Men . . .

Ring Out the Old, Ring in the
New

EASTER, PALM SUNDAY, PASSION WEEK, SPRING

The Day of Resurrection
All Glory, Laud, and Honor
Spring Has Now Unwrapped
Her Flowers
Come Ye Faithful, Raise the
Strain
With Face Set Steadfast Forward

Now the Spring Has Come
Again
Good Christian Men Rejoice and
Sing
The Strife Is O'er (v. 1, 3)
Ride On, Ride On in Majesty
Rejoice! The Lord Is King

THANKSGIVING

We Plow the Fields
Come, Ye Thankful People,
Come
For All the Blessings of the Year

Now Sing We a Song for the
Harvest
O God, Beneath Thy Guiding
Hand

CHRISTMAS

Angels We Have Heard on High
(Chorus)
Good Christian Men, Rejoice
Shepherds, Shake Off Your
Drowsy Sleep
Ring, O Ring, Ye Christmas
Bells
O Come, O Come, Emmanuel
Joy to the World
The First Noel

O Come, All Ye Faithful
Silent Night
While Shepherds Watched Their
Flocks by Night
God Rest Ye Merry, Gentlemen
Unto Us a Boy Is Born
What Child Is This
O Little Town of Bethlehem
I Heard the Bells on Christmas
Day

(For other traditional carols and many from other lands see:
Christmas Carols from Many Lands, Satis N. Coleman and E. K.
Jorgensen. New York: G. Schirmer, Inc., 1934.

PRAYER HYMNS

Spirit of Life in This New
Dawn

Gracious Spirit, Dwell with Me
Prayer Is the Soul's Sincere
Desire

Spirit of God, Descend Upon My Heart

Dear Lord and Father of Mankind

O God, Our Dwelling-Place

Now Thank We All Our God

O God, I Thank Thee for Each Sight

Be Thou My Vision

God of Grace and God of Glory

Now In the Days of Youth

RESPONSES AND INTROITS

We Give Thee but Thine Own

Be Present at Our Table, Lord (substitute "fellowship" for "paradise")

O Worship the Lord

The Lord Is in His Holy Temple

Hear Our Prayer, O Lord

All Things Come of Thee (two tunes)

The Lord Bless Us and Keep Us

Man Lives Not For Himself Alone . . .

Grant Us Lord, the Grace of Giving

Praise to the Lord!

Holy, Holy, Holy (*Sanctus* from Gaul's "The Holy City")

Day Is Dying in the West (Chorus only)

AMENS

Dresden

Sevenfold

Twofold

Threefold

PRELUDE MUSIC

In general for church school worship services the simplest and best preludes may be the good hymns of the church or chorales such as those by Bach.

MUSIC FOR CHILDREN'S CHOIRS

A few of the great hymns of the church are doubtless the best choices for children's choirs, such as:

We Thy People Praise Thee

All Creatures of Our God and King

Hear Us, Our Father

The World One Neighborhood, by Jeanette Perkins Brown

The Spacious Firmament on High

18.
Choral Speech

DRAMATIC AND SPECIAL WORSHIP SERVICES as well as parts of the regular formal worship of the church school lend themselves to group participation through choral speaking.

BOOKS TO INTERPRET CHORAL EXPRESSION

Gullan, Marjorie, *Choral Speaking*. Magnolia, Mass.: Expression Co., 1936.

————, *Poetry Speaking for Children*. Magnolia, Mass.: Expression Company.

McCullough, Grace A., *Speech Improvement Work and Practice Book*. Magnolia, Mass: Expression Co., 1960.

Swann, Mona, *An Approach to Choral Speech*. New York: Macmillan Co., 1946.

BIBLICAL MATERIALS FOR CHORIC USE IN WORSHIP

Psalm 19:1-4
Psalms 31:7, 33:5, 36:7, 9:1, 18:1, 36:7, 106:1 (in that order)
Psalms 98:4-6; 104:14, 24, 33; 107:2
Psalms 136:1-9, 25, 26; 139:14
Psalm 147:7-9, 16-18
Deuteronomy 33:13-16
See also "The Passion Week from Scripture," at the end of this chapter.

A HELPFUL SOURCE OF CHORIC READINGS

One of the best collections of materials for choric speaking is Jeanette P. Brown's *Children's Worship in the Church School* (New York: Harper & Row, 1939). Particularly recommended are the following:

"The Great World," William Brighty Rands (p. 21)
"The Earth Is Full of Thy Riches," Nancy Byrd Turner (p. 21)
"Yonder Is the Sea, Great and Wide," Nancy Byrd Turner (p. 22)
"St. Francis' Song of the Sun," translated by Sophie Jewett (p. 23)
"Thanksgiving Proclamation," by a third-grade class (p. 23)
"Wonderings" (p. 24)
"Beautiful Things," Nancy Byrd Turner (p. 26)
"Music," Harriet Cannon, age 8 (p. 28)
"Color," by a fifth-grade class (p. 29)
"A Children's Song" (p. 30)
"Winter Beauties," Florence M. Taylor (p. 30)
"Offering Verses" (p. 81)
"O Father" (p. 81)
"O God" (p. 82)
"The Greatest," Marion Brown Shelton (p. 105)
"The Friend of Everyone," Alice M. Pullen (p. 105)
"Our Dear Church Was Built" (p. 115)
"Walk Slowly" (p. 126)
"Ring of Love Around the World," Nancy Byrd Turner (p. 133)
"O God, Father of All Children" (p. 136)
"A Prayer to God" (p. 137)
"Father of All Children" (p. 166)

Poems

"To Be Alive in Such an Age," Angela Morgan
"Miracles," Walt Whitman
"Roadways," John Masefield
"Lines after Tea at Grasmere," William Wordsworth
"America for Me," Henry Van Dyke
"The Sacrament of Love," John Oxenham
"Holy Thursday," William Blake
"The Creation," James Weldon Johnson
"Now Every Child," Eleanor Farjeon
"The Shepherd's Song," Myles Connolly
"The Little Plant," Kate L. Brown

"Consider the Lilies," William C. Gannett
"Mary," Margaret E. Sangster

A Choric Reading on Forgiveness

SOLO VOICE (SOPRANO) :

The Lord is slow to anger, and abounding in steadfast love, forgiving iniquity and transgression (Numbers 14:18).

CHORUS:

Hearken thou to the supplications of thy servant, and of thy people, Israel, when they pray toward this place: yea, hear thou from heaven thy dwelling place! and when thou hearest, forgive (2 Chronicles 6:21).

SOLO VOICE (SOPRANO) :

For thou, O Lord, art good and forgiving, and abounding in steadfast love to all who call on thee (Psalm 86:5).

SOLO VOICE (BASS) :

If my people who are called by my name humble themselves, and pray and seek my face, and turn from their wicked ways, then I will hear from heaven, and will forgive their sin and heal their land (2 Chronicles 7:14).

CHORUS:

Bless the Lord, O my soul, and forget not all his benefits, who forgives all your iniquity, who heals all your diseases (Psalm 103: 2, 3).

SOLO VOICE (BASS) :

Let it be known to you therefore, brethren, that through this man forgiveness of sins is proclaimed to you (Acts 13:38).

SOLO VOICE (BARITONE) :

You have heard that it was said, "An eye for an eye and a tooth for a tooth." But I say to you, Do not resist one who is evil. But if any one strikes you on the right cheek, turn to him the other also; and if any one would sue you and take your coat, let him have your cloak as well; and if any one forces you to go one mile, go with him two miles. Give to him who begs from you, and do not refuse him who would borrow from you. You have heard that it was said, "You shall love your neighbor and hate your enemy." But I say to you, Love your enemies and pray for those who persecute you, so that you may be sons of your Father who is in heaven; for he makes his sun rise on the evil and on the good, and sends rain on the just and on the unjust. For if you love those who love you, what reward have you? Do not even the tax collectors do the same? And if you salute only your brethren, what more are you doing than others? Do not even the Gentiles do the same? (Matthew 5:38-47).

CHORUS:

You, therefore, must be perfect, as your Heavenly Father is perfect (Matthew 5:48).

CHORUS:

To the Lord our God belong mercy and forgiveness; because we have rebelled against him (Daniel 9:9). Hear thou in heaven, and forgive the sin of thy people (1 Kings 8:34a).

SOLO VOICE (BASS):

Take heed to yourselves: if your brother sins, rebuke him, and if he repents, forgive him; and if he sins against you seven times in the day, and turns to you seven times and says, "I repent," you must forgive him (Luke 17:3, 4).

MEN'S VOICES:

Lord, how often shall my brother sin against me, and I forgive him? As many as seven times? (Matthew 18:21b).

SOLO VOICE (BARITONE):

Jesus said: I do not say to you seven times, but seventy times seven (Matthew 18:22). Forgive, and you will be forgiven (Luke 6:37b); And whenever you stand praying, forgive, if you have anything against anyone (Mark 11:25a).

CHORUS:

That your Father also who is in heaven may forgive you your trespasses (Mark 11:25b).

A PASSION WEEK READING FROM SCRIPTURE

This message may be given by a verse-speaking choir:

CONSPIRACY

Luke 22:1, 2 [And Judas called Iscariot, a member of the twelve], Luke 22:4, 5, 6.

THE PASSOVER

Luke 22:7-14	Matt. 26:26-28a
Matt. 26:19, 20	John 15:8-14
John 13:4-17	Matt. 26:30-34, 35
John 13:21-30	

GETHSEMANE

Matt. 26:36-51, 55, 57a

HOUSE OF CAIAPHAS

Matt. 26:57b, 62-68	Mark 14:66-72

PILATE

Mark 15:1-19

CRUCIFIXION

Mark 15:20-32   Luke 23:34, 44-49

BURIAL

Luke 23:50-56   Matt. 27:62-66

RESURRECTION

I Corinthians 15:35-38; 15:42-44, 50
John 16:31-33   John 14:15-16

19.
Prayers for Teaching and Worship[1]

PRAYERS AT TABLE

God is great and God is good
And we thank him for our food.
By his hand we all are fed,
Give us, Lord, our daily bread. Amen

For health and strength and daily food
We give thee thanks, O Lord. Amen.

For all we eat, for all we wear,
For all the care of God our Father
We thank thee. Amen.

O God, we thank thee for good weather to grow our crops and we thank thee for people who harvest and sell food to us. We wish for more of thy spirit to work out a way to share our food with the starving people of other countries since we have enough for ourselves. Amen.

O God, we thank you for the food that we are about to receive. Thank you for the sunshine, rain, and soil that make it grow. We are grateful for our mothers, who cook our food. We wish more

[1] See bibliography, Chapter 14, for books of prayers.

of your help to learn to share it with people who do not have any. Fill our hearts with unselfish love. Amen.

O God, I am thankful for my mother and my father, for the food I have to eat and the clothes I have to wear and a house to keep me warm. Amen.

O God, we thank thee for our food and clothes and friends and teachers, our country and people. We also thank thee for the sun and the grass about our feet. Dear God, we thank thee for everything. Amen.

Singing Graces

Older children and young people can learn a variety of singing graces to use at camp, and at table in their own homes.

doxology

Praise God from whom all blessings flow;
Praise him all creatures here below;
Praise him above ye heavenly host;
Praise Father, Son and Holy Ghost. Amen.

tune: where cross the crowded ways of life

We thank thee for the morning light,
For rest and shelter of the night,
For health and food, for love and friends,
For everything thy goodness sends. Amen.

tune: for the beauty of the earth

For the beauty of the earth,
For the glory of the skies,
For this food which now we eat,
And for all good gifts besides:
Lord of all to thee we raise
This our hymn of grateful praise. Amen.

tune: take my life and let it be

Thou art great and thou art good,
And we thank thee for this food;
By thy hand must we be fed;
Give us, Lord, our daily bread. Amen.

TUNE: SUN OF MY SOUL, THOU SAVIOR DEAR

For food and health and happy days
Accept our gratitude and praise;
In serving others, Lord, may we
Repay our debt of love to thee.   Amen.

Selected Prayers

George Washington's Prayer

(Prayer made by George Washington at his inauguration in the Old Federal Building on the north side of Wall Street, facing Broad; this prayer has been framed and hangs in his pew in St. Paul's P.E. Chapel, Broad and Vesey Streets, New York City)

Almighty God, we make our earnest prayer that thou wilt keep the United States in thy holy protection; that thou wilt incline the hearts of the citizens to cultivate a spirit of subordination and obedience to government; to entertain a brotherly affection and love for one another and for their fellow citizens at large.

And finally that thou wilt most graciously be pleased to dispose us all to do justice, to love mercy and to demean ourselves with that charity, humility and pacific temper of mind, which were the characteristics of the Divine Author of our blessed religion, and without an humble imitation of whose example in all these things we can never hope to be a happy nation.

Grant our supplication, we beseech thee, through Jesus Christ, our Lord.   Amen.

A Young Man's Prayer

God, make of me a Christian man. Give me the strength to stand for right when other folks have left the fight. Give me the courage of the man who knows that if he will he can. Teach me to see in every face the good, the kind, and not the base. Make me sincere in word and deed. Blot out from me all sham and greed. Help me to guard my troubled soul by constant, active self-control. Clean up my thoughts, my speech, my play, and keep me pure from day to day. O make of me a Christian man.

A Soldier's Prayer on the Eve of Battle

Lord God, I have never spoken to you,
But now I want to say, "How do you do!"
You see, God, they told me you didn't exist,
And, like a fool, I believed all this.

Last night from a shell hole I saw your sky;
I figured right then they had told me a lie.
Had I taken time to see things you made,
I'd known that they weren't calling a spade a spade.
I wonder, God, if you'd shake my hand;
Somehow I feel that you'll understand.
Funny I had to come to this hellish place,
Before I had time to see your face.
Well, I guess there isn't much more to say,
But I'm sure glad that I met you today.
I guess the "zero hour" will soon be here,
But I'm not afraid, since I know you're near.
The signal! Well, God, I'll have to go,
I like you lots, this I want you to know.
Look, now, this will be a horrible fight.
Who knows? I may come to your house tonight.
Though I wasn't friendly to you before,
I wonder, God, if you'd wait at your door.
Look, I'm crying! Me shedding tears!
I wish I had known you these many years.
Well, I have to go now. Goodbye!
Strange, since I met you, I'm not afraid to die!

(Note: Anzio Beachhead, Italy. This poem was found on the body of one of our boys, written on the night before. It was copied by Norman T. Pennypacker, who fought by his side on this beachhead and forwarded it to one of his friends in America.[1]

A CHRISTMAS PRAYER

O God, most high, most lowly, the Holy One of our vision and dream, with happy hearts we worship thee in whose presence the greatest are but babes. High as the stars are above the earth are thy ways above our ways; yet didst thou make thyself as small as a little child lying down upon the doorstep of the world — a babe to break our heart and to mend it. By his grace, make us the child we never yet have been — free, trustful, and joyous of heart. As we bow at the cradle of Jesus, let there be in us, O Lord, a new nativity of faith and hope and the charity that thinketh no evil and abideth forever. May his gentleness touch us to a new gentleness toward all our fellow men in whom, however dimly, thou dwellest; and move us to a more liberal devising in behalf of

[1] Published in *The Leader*, Seaford, Delaware, Friday, June 30, 1944. Used by permission.

those who know bitterness and want. Freely we have received thy greatest gift. Freely may we give ourselves and our best gifts. Hasten the day, we pray thee, when the spirit of love and gladness shall fill the earth with shapes of purity and beauty, as of old it made the sky melodious with prophecy. Help forward the time when there shall be no more war, no more misery in our streets, because the laws of love have been searched out. Make our hearts a cradle of peace and good will toward men. Amen.

GENERAL CONFESSION

Almighty and most merciful Father; we have erred and strayed from thy ways like lost sheep. We have followed too much the devices and desires of our own hearts. We have offended against thy holy laws. We have left undone those things which we ought to have done; and we have done those things which we ought not to have done; and there is no health in us. But thou, O Lord, have mercy upon us, miserable offenders. Spare thou those, O God, who confess their faults. Restore thou those who are penitent, according to thy promises declared unto mankind in Christ Jesus our Lord. And grant, O most merciful Father, for his sake, that we may hereafter live a godly, righteous, and sober life, to the glory of thy holy Name. Amen.

A PRAYER — "FOR OUR EVIL-WILLERS"

(An old Elizabethan prayer, expressing in quaint but singularly relevant words the spirit of goodwill toward enemies, has been published by the International Fellowship of Reconciliation.)

Most merciful and loving Father, we beseech thee most humbly, even with all our hearts, to pour out upon our enemies with bountiful hands whatsoever things thou knowest may do them good: and chiefly a sound and uncorrupt mind, wherethrough they may know thee and seek thee in true charity, with their whole heart, and love us, thy children, for thy sake. Let not their first hating of us turn to their harm; neither let us in any wise hurt them, seeing that we cannot do them good for want of ability. Lord, we desire their amendment, and not their punishment. Separate them not from us by punishing them, but join and knit them to us by thy favorable dealing with them. And seeing we be all ordained to be citizens of the one everlasting city, let us begin to enter into that way here already by mutual love, which may bring us right forth thither.[2]

[2] Used by permission of the International Fellowship of Reconciliation.

INVOCATION

Almighty and everlasting God, in whom we live and move and have our being, who hast created us for thyself, so that our hearts are restless until they find rest in thee, grant unto us purity of heart and strength of purpose, so that no selfish passion may hinder us from knowing thy will, and no weakness from doing it. In thy light may we see life clearly, and in thy service find perfect freedom. For thy mercy's sake. Amen.

PAX VOBISCUM

Friend, you have come to this church; leave it not without a prayer. No man entering a house ignores him who dwells in it. This is the house of God and he is here.

Pray then to him who loves you and bids you welcome and awaits your greeting.

Give thanks for those who in past ages built this place to his glory and for those who, dying that we might live, have preserved for us our heritage.

Praise God for his gifts of beauty in painting and architecture, handicraft and music.

Ask that we who now live may build the spiritual fabric of the nation in truth, beauty, and goodness; and that, as we draw near to the one Father through our Lord and Savior Jesus Christ, we may draw nearer to one another in perfect brotherhood.

The Lord preserve thy going out and thy coming in.

PRAYER FOR OUR COUNTRY

O God of freedom, under thy guiding hand our pilgrim fathers crossed the sea. We rejoice that in thy spirit they founded a nation dedicated to liberty, equality, and the brotherhood of man. We thank thee . . . for their daring experiment in the untried ways of government by the people.

Give to us, we pray, the spirit of the fathers as we, too, face a new world. Give us their faith and courage to launch . . . such new forms as may be necessary to fulfill the purposes for which our country came to birth. . . . Help us . . . to extend . . . freedom for the common man. . . .

May we also go forward in the spirit of divine adventure into the new world of international relations. Through cooperative institutions . . . may we play our part in . . . order to establish justice among the nations, assure peace . . . in all the world and promote the general welfare of mankind. . . . God of our fathers, be with us yet. Amen.[3]

A PRAYER OF ST. BASIL (379 A.D.)

O Lord our God, teach us, we beseech thee, to ask thee aright. . . . Show us the course wherein we should go. . . . Let thy Spirit curb our wayward senses, and guide . . . us into that which is our true good, to keep thy laws, and in thy glorious . . . presence. For thine is the . . . praise . . . for ever and ever, Amen.[4]

A PRAYER BY CHRISTINA G. ROSSETTI

O faithful Lord, grant to . . . us . . . faithful hearts devoted to thee, and to the service of all men for thy sake. Fill us with pure love of thee; keep us steadfast in this love . . . . Amen.[5]

A PRAYER FOR WORKERS

O God, we thank thee for men and women all over this world who work that we may have health, food, clothing, and good times. We thank thee for those who work in dangerous mines, for those who work on machines, for those who sail on the ships, and for those who tend great furnaces in our factories. We thank thee for those who plant and gather our food, for those who care for dairies that give us clean and wholesome milk, and for all those who live as migrants and care for the crops that mean so much to us as food. We thank thee for those who keep homes, for those who train children. We are sorry for those who are underpaid, for those who have little time to play, for those who are unkind and selfish towards people who work for them. O God of us all, we would work more with thee to bring love and kindness into the world where people work. Amen.

A MODERN LORD'S PRAYER

Dear God, the Father of everyone, we would use your name reverently.
May we live as you want us to, a way of love and fairness so that

[3] James Myers, *Prayers for Self and Society* (New York: Association Press, 1934).

[4] From *Prayers, Ancient and Modern,* ed. by Mary W. Tileston (New York: Grosset & Dunlap, 1949), p. 55.

[5] *Ibid.,* p. 142.

there may be peace in the world, not war. And may we share what we have with those who have less, so that no one will be without food and shelter and medical care.

We are sorry when we do unfair, mean, and selfish things which hurt other people. And help us, we pray, to forget when others hurt us.

Help us, too, our Father, not even to think of doing anything we know is wrong.

For the wonder, the beauty, the love and goodness in your world, we give our thanks and praise. Amen.[6]

GRACE AT LUNCHEON

O God, whose love is over all, we would remind ourselves of some of the many people who have worked in school, in field, in laboratory, in factory, in stores; on busses, planes, and trains; in kitchens and in endless other services to provide us with this meal today. We thank thee for these children of thine, for their weary labor and for their patient skills. Now we would thank thee for this time of communion together. May we break this bread in loving fellowship. May we go forth strengthened to enter more fully in cooperation with thee and with one another. Amen.

— *Edna M. Baxter*

PRAYER BY RABINDRANATH TAGORE

This is my prayer to
    Thee, my Lord —
Give me the strength lightly
    to bear my joys and sorrows.
Give me the strength to make
    my love fruitful in service.
Give me the strength never
    to disown the poor or bend
    my knees before insolent might.
Give me the strength to
    raise my mind above daily trifles.
Give me the strength to surrender
    my strength to thy will with love.[7]

[6] Written by young people in the First Church of Christ, Congregational, West Hartford, Conn.)

[7] Reprinted with permission of the publisher from *Gitanjali*, by Rabindranath Tagore. Copyright 1918 by The Macmillan Company, renewed in 1946 by Rabindranath Tagore.

THE ONE THOUSANDTH PSALM

O God, we thank thee for everything!

For the sea and its waves, blue, green, and gray and always wonderful;

For the beach and the breakers and the spray and the white foam on the rocks;

For the blue arch of heaven; for the clouds in the sky, white and gray and purple;

For the green of the grass; for the forests in their spring beauty; for the wheat and corn and rye and barley;

For the brown earth turned up by the plow, for the sun by day, and the dews by night;

We thank thee for all thou hast made and that thou hast called it good.

For all the glory and beauty and wonder of the world;

For the glory of springtime, the tints of the flowers and their fragrance;

For the glory of the summer flowers, the roses and cardinals and clethra;

For the glory of the autumn, the scarlet and crimson and gold of the forest;

For the glory of winter, the pure snow on the shrubs and trees.

We thank thee that thou hast placed us in the world to subdue all things to thy glory.

And to use all things for the good of thy children.

We thank thee! We enter into thy work, and go about thy business.

— Edward Everett Hale

A UNISON PRAYER

We would find thee, O God, in the hearts and lives of the men, women, and children that are all about us. May we break down every barrier that hinders us from really knowing one another. Bring us together, we pray thee, in friendly intimacies, in mutual enjoyments and in common aspirations. Let those who are privileged bring gifts of leisure and culture. Let the distressed and the unsatisfied bring gifts of eagerness and desire. Let the powerful lift up the weak, and the lighthearted bring comfort to the overburdened. Though we come from the ends of society, and are separated by injustice, prejudice, and untoward circumstance, help us, O God, to seek out one another in love and patience and to rest not until, through fellowship and friendliness, we have realized a large measure of the relationship of brothers and sisters of a common Father.

PRAYER FOR THE NEW YEAR

O Lord, make me an instrument of thy peace; where there is hatred, let me sow love; where there is injury, pardon; where there is doubt, faith; where there is despair, hope; where there is darkness, light; and where there is sadness, joy.

O Divine Master, grant that I may not so much seek to be consoled as to console; to be understood as to understand; to be loved as to love; for it is in giving that we receive, it is in pardoning that we are pardoned, and it is in dying that we are born to eternal life.

— *St. Francis of Assisi*

THE HIGHER PATRIOTISM

O God, thou great governor of all the world, we pray thee for all who hold public office and power, for the life, the welfare, and the virtue of the people are in their hands to make or mar. We remember with shame that in the past the mighty have preyed on the labors of the poor; they have laid nations in the dust by their oppression, and have thwarted the love and the prayers of thy servants. . . .

Strengthen the sense of duty in our political life . . . . Purge our cities and states and nations of the deep causes of corruption which have so often made sin profitable and uprightness hard . . . . Give our leaders a new vision of the possible future of our country and set their hearts on fire with large resolves. Raise up a new generation of public men, who will have the faith and daring of the kingdom of God in their hearts, and who will enlist for life in a holy warfare for the freedom and rights of the people.

—*Walter Rauschenbusch*[8]

PRAYER FOR PEACE

O God, who hast made of one blood all nations of men to dwell on the face of the whole earth, and who of old didst send forth thy messengers to prepare the way of the Lord; grant that all men

[8] *Prayers of the Social Awakening*, by Walter Rauschenbusch (Boston: The Pilgrim Press, 1925), pp. 79, 80. Used by permission.

everywhere may seek after thee and find thee. Bring the nations into thy fold, and hasten thy kingdom. Prepare our hearts to receive thy truth in the love of it. May the truth make us free from the bondage of error and evil with the glorious liberty of the children of God. May the fruit be unto holiness, and the end the life that is life indeed. Grant us to share with the earnest souls of all the ages that desire for peace that shall lead us to a living fellowship with the Prince of Peace. Amen.

PRAYER FOR HOMES

Almighty God, we thank thee for the comforts and joys of the home and for human friendship and love. We pray that thy spirit may ever dwell in our households and make us all true to our relations and duties one to another. Enable us to perform our tasks well, to meet our trials bravely, to enjoy our pleasures thankfully, and to bear our disappointments patiently, so that our labors and our examples may be profitable to others and we may all be true servants of our Lord and Master, Jesus Christ. Keep us, we pray thee, from anger and strife, from envy and selfishness. Make us loyal in our affections and cheerful in our fellowship. Bless all whom we love and all who belong to us, wherever they are today. Increase the spirit of peace and brotherly kindness throughout the world, and grant us grace daily to do something for the coming of that blessed day when all households of earth shall belong to the great family of God and render praises and glory unto the Father, the Son, and the Holy Ghost. Amen. — *Henry Van Dyke*[9]

ADORATION

O God, we joyfully come before thee in adoration and with praise. All thy works surround us. Earth and heaven reflect thy power and thy truth.

Because thou hast shown us the glory of thy kingdom in the prophets and in the majestic love of Jesus Christ, we adore thee.

Because, O God, thou art always working in the world through thy mighty and loving spirit, we adore thee.

We bless thee for our creation and preservation in this life.

We praise thee for all thy servants who by their example and leadership have helped us on our way.

Once again we would dedicate our will and our spirit to thy eternal and glorious purpose, and in the spirit of Jesus Christ. Amen. — *Edna M. Baxter*

[9] Used by permission of Mrs. Tertius Van Dyke.

A CLOSING PRAYER

Give us, O Lord, love that embraces all, sympathy that always understands, patience that never flags, loyalty that cannot play false. Strengthen our wills, that we may choose the right way even when it is the hard way. Liberate us from the tyranny of evil, that neither persons nor things can vitiate our judgments or enslave our purposes. You who are the Best, mold us after the pattern of yourself until we are your friends and the friends of all kinds of people. Amen.

20.
Some Ideas
for Worship Services

ALREADY WE HAVE EMPHASIZED that effective worship should follow the work period and group meeting of the class, serving as a climax to the whole session, gathering up important religious meanings from the session and relating them to the present-day outlook of the students. If periods are brief, there may be time for only a prayer and a closing hymn. Some sessions will serve as a climax to a given study or group of lessons, with a play or a program, together with choric readings, prayers, and hymns.

In the materials that follow, one complete formal service is included as a suggestion for the arrangement of others. Attention is called to this order, which places Scripture after concrete material given in a talk or a story and follows with prayer as the climax. It is helpful to have a series of services on one theme, or to conduct a climax service after a series of studies. Decide where these services will fit best into your teaching.

The service which begins on the next page is formal in nature and is designed with teen-agers in mind. A similar outline, with different content, could be used for children.

213

OVERCOMING EVIL WITH GOOD

1. Processional: "Joyful, Joyful, We Adore Thee"
2. Unison Call to Worship:
   God is a Spirit, and they that worship him must worship him in Spirit and in truth.
   God is love, and he that dwelleth in love dwelleth in God and God in him.
3. Sanctus:
   Holy, Holy, Holy, Lord of hosts;
   Holy, Holy, Holy is the Lord of hosts. Amen
4. Story: "Mr. Gandhi Discovered the Power of Love."
5. Read chorically: I Cor. 13:6-8.
6. Prayer of Thanksgiving for God's plan as discovered by Mr. Gandhi and by Paul.
7. Hymn: "O God Whose Love Is over All."

MR. GANDHI DISCOVERED THE POWER OF LOVE

How shocking it must have been for the very well-educated Indian lawyer, recently home as a graduate from Oxford University, to find when traveling in Africa that he would not be allowed to sit in a train with white people. He had received his education in England and then had come home to India to set up a law practice; but, just as he was beginning it, he received a call from some Indians in Natal, Africa, to come to that province to help them. The white people in South Africa were trying to take away the privilege of voting from the Indians who had gone there from India, and they needed his good legal training to help them.

After much deliberation the young lawyer, whose name was Gandhi, started on that long journey. When he arrived in Africa he naturally bought a first class ticket for the train to Natal, for he was an able, educated, and cultured man. Upon boarding the train he soon noticed, however, some condescending glances were thrown his way. He had ignored them until the conductor came to his seat and asked who he was and why he was in that car! Mr. Gandhi was astonished and puzzled. He showed the conductor his ticket and said that he had purchased a first-class reservation. This seemed to make no difference to the conductor, who demanded that Mr. Gandhi leave this segregated car for white people. He was ordered into a crowded, dirty car where all Indians were required to ride, third class. At his refusal the conductor picked him up and dragged him into the car. The rich, educated, cultured lawyer,

Mr. Gandhi, was learning fast why the Indian people in Africa had sent for him.

When he reached Natal, he was very much hurt and homesick. He was a stranger in a strange land, and he missed the friends and luxury which he had enjoyed both in England and at his own home. However, he went to the Grand Hotel because he had always gone to the best hotels. On his arrival the people only laughed when he asked for a room and ridiculed him for expecting to stay in a place kept only for white people. Mr. Gandhi didn't know what next to do; he had no idea where he could spend the night. As he began to pray, however, asking God to show him the way, he met an Indian friend who said, "I know a white woman who is a Christian and I believe she will be pleased to take you to her home." By this time Mr. Gandhi was glad to go to a friendly place. Here he did indeed find a kindly welcome. This Christian home then became his home all the while he was in Natal.

Mr. Gandhi discovered that the treatment of the Indians in Natal was very cruel. When Indians walked on the streets and met a white person, they were forced to leave it and to walk in the road. If they got in the way of the white man, they were kicked out of the way — much as some people kick at strange dogs that are in their way. No Indians were allowed on the streets after nine o'clock at night. Probably the reason white men had such laws was that they were so cruel to the Indians that they feared revenge after dark.

Indian friends of Mr. Gandhi begged him to stay in South Africa and help them to get more freedom. They wanted to start a revolt. While Gandhi was deciding what to do, the Christian woman with whom he lived gave him a Bible to read. Mr. Gandhi became greatly interested in it. He read about Jesus, who taught man to love his enemies and to do good to those who wrong him. Gandhi was astonished to read, "I say unto you that ye resist not evil, but whosoever shall slap you on the right cheek, turn to him the other also," and "Love your enemies, bless them that curse you, do good to them that hate you, and pray for them which despitefully use you, that you may be the children of your Father who is in heaven."

Mr. Gandhi thought a long time about these teachings. He realized that the Indians would not have a possible chance to get their freedom if they went to war with the English people, because they would not have the materials for war. The resistance that Jesus taught sounded much wiser. Finally Mr. Gandhi decided to give up his law practice in India, and sent for his family. He would stay in South Africa where he could teach his people this wonderful thing, the *power* of love.

Gradually the Indians began to realize what he meant by loving everyone, and even some of the white men became impressed by his use of love to bring about better conditions. As a result, Mr. Gandhi was able to do more for the Indians than he could ever have done had he led them in a rebellion.

Finally he went back to India to lead his people there to seek freedom from British rule. This discovery of love as a way of life made him one of the most powerful and helpful men in all of India. The British put him and his friends in prison many times; but, through meditation and prayer instead of guns and bombs, Mr. Gandhi helped lead multitudes of his people to struggle for their freedom in a new way. Eventually, without guns or hate, the powerful British Empire gave India its independence.

CONCRETE MATERIALS FOR OTHER WORSHIP SERVICES

At the present hour man's inhumanity towards his fellows reveals how slowly people learn to live under the rule of God and his more eternal and triumphant laws of life. The struggle for freedom with its attendant individual responsibilities is evident on a world scale today. Young folks should face its meaning in concrete terms. Abstract words about love and goodness are only meaningful as they are put to work and understood in concrete events and in relation to actual people.

Current situations cannot easily be put in a book. The teacher is urged to use the following addresses to seek sources of incidents in human relations and stories of constructive things being done to improve human life and human situations. Help the students to realize that human beings are God's most precious creation.

The Fellowship of Reconciliation
North Broadway
Upper Nyack, N. Y.

National Association for the Advancement of Colored People
20 West 40th Street
New York, N. Y.

Council for Christian Social Action
United Church of Christ
297 Park Ave. South
New York, N. Y.

Congress of Racial Equality
38 Park Row
New York, N. Y.

National Conference of Christians and Jews
43 West 57th Street
New York, N. Y.

American Friends Service Committee
160 North 15th Street
Philadelphia, Pa.

National Council of the Churches of Christ in the U. S. A.
475 Riverside Drive
New York, N. Y.

National Division of Home Missions
National Council of Churches
475 Riverside Drive
New York, N. Y.

Write to the social action offices of the Presbyterian, United Church, Methodist, Episcopal, Baptist, and other denominations for illustrations of situations to be worked on in improving race, labor, and other human relations.

Look for incidents aiding people to live more justly, to get work, to be properly fed, clothed and housed, to have better medical care, to have freedom and equality of opportunity.

Find out what is being done by churches to improve the life of the Puerto Ricans, Spanish-Americans, Indians, migrants, Japanese-Americans, Negroes, and other minorities.

Services to Use at the Conclusion of Discussions

THEME I. ARE WE OUR BROTHER'S KEEPERS?

1. Read chorically or by a prepared individual:

In most ways all races and kinds of people are alike. God created them "in his own image."   — Genesis 1:27

And he made from one every nation of men to live on all the face of the earth.

— *Acts 17:26*

See what love the Father has given us, that we should be called children of God; and so we are.

— *1 John 3:1*

Paul said, "Decide never to put a stumbling block or hindrance in the way of a brother."

— *Romans 14:13b*

> There is a destiny that makes us brothers;
> None goes his way alone:
> All that we send into the lives of others
> Comes back into our own.
>
> — *Edwin Markham* [1]

This moment yearning and thoughtful sitting alone,
It seems to me there are other men in other lands
 yearning and thoughtful,
It seems to me that I can look over and behold them
 in Germany, Italy, France, Spain,
Or far, far away, in China, or in Russia or Japan,
 talking other dialects,
And it seems to me if I could know
 those men, I should become attached
 to them as I do to men in my own lands,
O I know we should be brethren and lovers,
I know I should be happy with them.

— *Walt Whitman* [2]

2. Prayer:
 Express regrets in particular ways for failures to act as brothers:
 "O God, we are sorry that we have been so rude to people in our school; we are sorry . . . [etc.] O God, we will try to think how it feels when people are treated rudely. We will try . . . [etc.]"

3. Hymn: "O God, Whose Love Is Over All."

[1] First verse of "The Creed." Used by permission of Virgil Markham.
[2] From *Leaves of Grass* (Garden City: Doubleday & Company, 1954), p. 131.

Use incidents in the treatment of races, other religious groups, and of individuals to show the need of being responsible in helping one another. Continue the above scripture and hymn for the series.

THEME II. NO ONE CAN LIVE TO HIMSELF

1. Group reads from a poster, or a prepared leader may read:

All your strength is in your union,
All your danger is in discord.
>— *Henry Wadsworth Longfellow*

Brethren, if a man is overtaken in any trespass, you who are spiritual should restore him in a spirit of gentleness. Look to yourself, lest you too be tempted. Bear one another's burdens, and so fulfill the law of Christ.
>— *Galatians 6:1, 2*

Behold, how good and pleasant it is
when brothers dwell in unity.
>— *Psalm 133:1*

Whoever would be first among you must be slave of all.
>— *Mark 10:44*

Jesus said: "By this all men will know that you are my disciples, if you have love for one another.
>— *John 13:35*

2. Give a series of talks on this theme, using such data as:
Gaining world peace by nations seeking the welfare of one another. Get information from the United Nations.
William Penn's Covenant.
Interdependence of nations and peoples.

3. Prayer — Guided meditations. "Let us close our eyes and think with God about how the Indians might have felt to be treated with such kindness." Silence. "Now ask God to be with you in some hard situation." In conclusion, oral prayer by leader.

4. Hymn: "These Things Shall Be: A Loftier Race."

THEME III. FORGETTING OURSELVES

(To close a class or meeting)

1. Readings placed on a poster to be read by the class:
Paul said, "I bid every one among you not to think of himself more highly than he ought to think."

— Romans 12:3

We know that in everything God works for good with those who love him."

— Romans 8:28

Paul told the Roman Christians: "Love one another with brotherly affection. . . . Rejoice in your hope, be patient in tribulation, be constant in prayer. Live in harmony with one another — do not be haughty, but associate with the lowly; never be self-conceited."

— Selections from Romans 12:10-16

We who are strong ought to bear with the failings of the weak, and not to please ourselves; let each of us please his neighbor, for his good, to edify him."

— Romans 15:1, 2

2. Prayer: Follow ideas in the readings.

3. Hymn: "Where Cross the Crowded Ways of Life."

CONTINUATION OF THEME III

Other services using this theme and these readings may present stories of people who have lived to help others. See *Prophet in the Wilderness,* by Hermann Hagedorn *(op. cit.),* and *Gandhi* by Jeanette Eaton *(op. cit.).*

THEME IV. DO WE WORK FOR A BETTER WORLD?

1. Readings after concreteness: Amos 5:24, Micah 4:1-4 and Micah 5:8

Observe good faith and justice toward all nations; cultivate peace and harmony with all. It will be worthy of a free, enlightened, and a great nation, to give to mankind the example of a people always guided by an exalted justice and benevolence.

— George Washington

2. Read or sing the words in unison as a prayer:
   Cure thy children's warring madness,
     Bend our pride to thy control;
   Shame our wanton, selfish gladness,
     Rich in things and poor in soul.
   Grant us wisdom,
   Grant us courage,
   Lest we miss thy kingdom's goal.
                                  — *Harry Emerson Fosdick* [3]

3. Closing Hymn: "God Send Us Men." (Tune: *Melrose*).

CONTINUATION OF THEME IV

Other services on this theme may report incidents on what is being done (1) to improve race relations; (see *Naught for Your Comfort*, by Trevor Huddleston, *op. cit.*), (2) to improve treatment of Jews, (3) to help migrants, etc.

THEME V. SHOULD WE LOVE OUR ENEMIES?

1. Readings after concreteness: Matthew 5:44-48 and Matthew 18:15; Galatians 6:1, 2; Ephesians 4:31, 32.

   Do not be overcome by evil, but overcome evil with good.
                                  — *Romans 12:21*

   I will show you a still more excellent way. . . . Love is patient and kind; love is not jealous or boastful; it is not arrogant or rude. Love does not insist on its own way; it is not irritable or resentful. It does not rejoice at wrong, but rejoices in the right.
                                  — *1 Corinthians 12:31b; 13:4-6*
   "And love the offender, yet detest the offense."
                                  — *Alexander Pope* [4]

2. Pray together the old Elizabethan Prayer (p. 205):

3. Hymn: "O God Whose Love Is Over All."

CONTINUATION OF THEME V

Other services on this theme using the same scripture may illustrate this. Use the story of Mei Ling.

[3] From "God of Grace and God of Glory." Used by permission of Harry Emerson Fosdick.

[4] *Eloise to Abelard*, by Alexander Pope, line 192.

MEI LING

A True Story from China

This is the story of Mei Ling, a seventeen-year-old village girl who lived in a remote country area of China in the 1930's. We have a mutual friend, she and I, a well-known British doctor, who gave me permission to tell this. As he got up from the table where he had been holding us spellbound with this story, he said, "It was one of the greatest spiritual experiences of my life."

Mei Ling heard that a school was being set up near her village by the foreign friends who lived five miles away. She soon learned to read and write five hundred of the difficult Chinese characters, and before long was making herself useful in helping the other scholars, men, women and girls. The war had been going on for more than a year, but the farmers and peasants of this village could not believe that the Japanese soldiers would ever reach them. Whenever they were warned of danger they would say, "Oh! such things will not happen here."

But one day the wind blew from a different quarter. They heard the machine gun fire. Soon a stream of refugees began trekking through the village, helping along their wounded and carrying bedding and babies. Now they started preparations. Mei Ling's father heard how the soldiers usually seized as many women and girls as they wanted, and one of the three chief reasons for the high death rate among non-combatants was that the men who tried to protect their women folk were bayoneted. He couldn't afford to be killed. What would the rest of the family, the younger children do? So he called his daughter to him and said, "You must make a plan for yourself." She understood that that meant, "Get out."

Some ten miles away there was a little clinic run by two Chinese men who were working under the direction of my doctor friend. Mei Ling walked over there and offered her services as a volunteer. They were glad to have her. She was quick to notice what needed to be done and did it cheerfully.

After a few weeks the Japanese soldiers were nearing the clinic, and the men who ran it knew what would happen to them if they tried to protect Mei Ling from their lust. So they, too, said to her, "You must make a plan for yourself." As they expected she would jump down the well, they made a noise at their work and talked loudly; they liked Mei Ling and did not want to hear the splash. But there was no splash. Mei Ling went a little way away, cut off her hair, dressed herself like a man, put on big farmer's boots, assumed a deep voice, and then came back and asked for a coolie's job at the clinic. The men were glad of help and wondered where the coolie had come from. When they found how clever their new helper was with the patients, they recognized Mei Ling but said nothing.

When the Japanese soldiers arrived, they brought in their wounded and ordered the Chinese to treat them. All day long Mei Ling worked hard washing wounds, bandaging limbs, giving anesthetics — while a pistol was held to her head by a Japanese soldier in case she ill-treated one of her country's enemies. At sundown the Japanese went away and barricaded themselves in their own camp, taking their wounded with them. (This was the regular custom in much of the Japanese-occupied area of China, where after sunset the Chinese came out from their hiding, carried on their business, made their plans, and settled their little affairs till daybreak.) The three clinic workers were glad to be alone. They wanted food and sleep. "What will our fellow-countrymen do to us tonight when they find we've been nursing the enemy?" asked one. "Kill us, probably," said another. "Let's go to sleep now in any case," said Mei Ling. And they did. Soon they were awakened by a great bang on the door. They picked up the lantern and went out to meet whatever awaited them. They opened the door and there stood the Chinese soldiers with their wounded, waiting for their help. "Come in," they cried gladly. And all night long they worked on their own people.

Before dawn the Chinese went off, and in the morning back came the Japanese. This went on for six weeks. One Sunday morning at the hospital fifteen miles away, the doctor who was giving the address saw a strange-looking creature seated — not on the right among the men, not on the left among the women, but all alone in the passage between. Was it a woman or a man? Somehow the creature looked familiar and very intelligent, and occasionally smiled and nodded at the doctor when he made a good point. He could not remember where he had seen such a person before. He kept fumbling for his next word as he taxed his memory. When the service was over he inquired who or what was sitting in the middle of the church.

"Don't you remember Mei Ling, the girl who learned to read so quickly?" asked the teacher, and he gave the doctor an account of her adventures.

"But if she's working under the Japanese in the clinic fifteen miles away, how did she get here?" inquired the doctor.

"They had run out of chloroform and anti-tetanus. Mei Ling knew we had plenty here, so she came along and climbed over our wall last night," answered the teacher.

"What courage," exclaimed the doctor, "to come five miles through Japanese, five miles through Chinese, and another five miles through Japanese territory alone!"

"Yes! None of the men would come, so she had to," added the teacher.

"I want to see her at once. Can I?" asked the doctor. But Mei Ling could not be found. Having got her supply of chloroform and anti-tetanus, she had climbed over the wall and started the return journey.

It was some months later when the doctor saw Mei Ling again. Many battles had raged since then, and many villages had been liquidated, Mei Ling's among them. No member of her family was left alive.

The town near the clinic had been taken by the Japanese, recovered by the Chinese, and retaken several times. The Japanese had shut down the clinic, and the town was in their hands when the doctor visited it. He noticed that an old missionary compound had been turned into a refugee camp. "Who was responsible for this?" he wondered, and went to inspect it. He found one hundred and fifty families enjoying safety here, also their livestock, pigs, fowl, and cattle. Everything was very orderly. No refugees seemed to be idle. They were organized so that each took his turn in the cooking, cleaning, and other work of the camp. Educational classes were being held also, and handicrafts carried on.

It was some time before the doctor found the person in charge. It was seventeen-year-old Mei Ling, the coolie. She was overjoyed to see him, and they had much to say to each other. She asked him to lead the evening prayer that night, but he wanted to be led by her, so he said that he would rather sit with the people and let the usual procedure be followed.

When the large assembly gathered together, men seated on the right, women on the left, Mei Ling stood up and read aloud some written prayers. Among the petitions was one that God would bless and comfort the Japanese who were probably suffering as refugees, many of them just as the Chinese were. Then she put down the printed paper and made up her own closing prayer,

"Oh, Lord, please help us to root out of our hearts all pride and

anger and fear because we know these are the things that make
wars."

— *Muriel Lester* [5]

THEME VI. WE BECOME LIKE OUR THOUGHTS

1. Readings after the concreteness:

"A man is what he thinks about" (Ralph Waldo Emerson).

Paul said: "Do not be conformed to this world, but be transformed by the renewal of your mind, that you may prove what
is the will of God, what is good and acceptable and perfect"
(Romans 12:2).

Paul wrote to the Christians at Philippi: "Finally, brethren,
whatever is true, whatever is honorable, whatever is just, whatever is pure, whatever is lovely, whatever is gracious, if there
is any excellence, if there is anything worthy of praise, think
about these things" (Philippians 4:8).

Think truly, and thy thoughts
    Shall the world's famine feed;
Speak truly, and each word of thine
    Shall be a fruitful seed;
Live truly, and thy life shall be
    A great and noble creed.

— *Horatius Bonar*

2. Prayer: Based on ideas in the readings.

3. Closing Hymn: "All Creatures of Our God and King" or "We
Would Be Building."

CONTINUATION OF THEME VI

Another service on this theme could use Hawthorne's story of
"The Great Stone Face" in condensed form. See also "My Dear
Ego" by Fritz Kunkel, (Philadelphia: United Church Press, 1947).

THEME VII. HOW TO GIVE

1. Readings after concreteness:

Paul wrote to the Christians at Corinth: "Each one must do as

[5] Used by permission of the International Fellowship of Reconciliation.

he has made up his mind, not reluctantly or under compulsion, for God loves a cheerful giver."

— 2 Corinthians 9:7b

If I give away all I have and I deliver my body to be burned, but have not love, I gain nothing.

— 1 Corinthians 13:3

Jesus' teachings — Matthew 6:1-4 and Mark 12:41-44.

2. Closing Prayer:

God of love,
We pray thee this day for the poor and outcast of this land;
For those who from year's end to year's end
Have never enough for their body's need:
For those who live perpetually on the bitter edge of starvation;
For those whose lot is continually shame and oppression,
Who for no fault of their own are loathed and spat upon;
For those who labor incessantly,
In heat and in thirst, for a miserable reward;
For those who are driven through want to shame and sin;
For those who have no hope in this life or beyond;
For those who labor helplessly for cruel masters . . .
And we ask thee for a share of thy spirit,
That we may give ourselves, gladly and generously,
In the constant endeavor to rescue and to emancipate
These, the needy and helpless ones of our nation —
These without whom she cannot be saved.[6]

3. Closing Hymn: "For the Workers"

CONTINUATION OF THEME VII

Other services using this theme and the readings may be built around service enterprises being carried on by the class or people of the denomination.

THEME VIII

STRUGGLING TOWARD FREEDOM FOR ALL PEOPLE

Note: Use model of Statue of Liberty for center of worship.

1. Story of the Indian Chief, below.

[6] *A Book of Prayers,* by J. S. Hoyland (New York: Association Press, 1939), p. 84.

2. Readings after concreteness:

One God and Father of us all, who is above all, and through all and in you all.

— *Ephesians 4:6*

God created man in his own image, in the image of God he created him.

— *Genesis 1:27*

Suggestions for application:
The poem on the Statue of Liberty
Questions from the Bill of Rights in the Constitution of the United States

3. Prayer

4. Closing Hymn: "America the Beautiful" or "These Things Shall Be"

CONTINUATION OF THEME VIII

Students may find stories of freedom in their school books and in newspaper accounts of the struggles of Negroes, American Indians, and the people of places like Hungary, Poland and Africa.

THE INDIAN CHIEF

Chief Joseph, of the Nez Perce tribe of Indians in Oregon, on the occasion of his being forced by our Government to retire to the reservation, said:

"If the white man wants to live in peace with the Indian, he can live in peace. There need be no trouble. Treat all men alike. Give them all the same law. Give them all an even chance to live and to grow. All men were made by the same Great Spirit Chief. They are all brothers. The earth is the mother of all people, and all people should have equal rights upon it. . . . If you tie a horse to a stake, do you expect him to grow fat? If you pen up an Indian on a small spot of earth and compel him to stay there, he will not be contented, nor will he grow and prosper. I have asked some of the great white chiefs where they get their authority to say to the Indian he shall stay on one place, while he sees white men going where they please. They cannot tell me.

"When I think of our conditions, my heart is heavy. I see men of my race treated as outlaws and driven from country to country or shot down like animals.

"We can only ask an even chance to live as other men live. . . .
Let me be a free man . . . free to travel, free to stop, free to
work, free to trade where I choose, free to choose my own teachers,
free to follow the religion of my fathers, free to think and to talk.
. . . and I will obey every law or submit to the penalty.

"Whenever the white man treats the Indian as the white men
treat one another, then we shall have no more wars. We shall be
brothers. Then the Great Spirit Chief who rules above will smile
upon this land, and send rain to wash out the bloody spots made
by brothers' hands from the face of the earth."

THEME IX
CHRISTMAS — "PEACE ON EARTH, GOODWILL TO MEN"

1. Readings after concreteness:

> I like to think that Jesus played
> And tumbled, wrestled, ran —
> That he was long a merry boy
> Before he was a man.
>
> He once was just the age I am
> And learned from teachers stern;
> He long was just a thoughtful lad,
> Before he taught, in turn.
>
> I like to know he toiled beside
> His father at his bench;
> His boyish fingers, calloused, bruised,
> Learned how things were made.
>
> I like to think that Jesus planned
> Through long, long youthful years,
> How he could help the helpless world
> And wipe away its tears.
>
> It helps me understand him when
> I know he was a small
> And gleeful boy, before he grew
> To be the Christ of all!
>
> —*Earl Bigelow*[7]

2. Prayer—Litany or Thanksgiving Prayer for Jesus' life.

[7] *Beacon Song and Service Book* (Boston: Beacon Press, 1960).

3. Closing Hymn: "I Heard the Bells on Christmas Day."

> I heard the bells on Christmas Day
> Their old familiar carols play,
> And wild and sweet the words repeat
> Of peace on earth, goodwill to men!
>
> I thought how, as the day had come,
> The belfries of all Christendom
> Had rolled along th' unbroken song
> Of peace on earth, goodwill to men!
>
> Till, ringing, singing on its way,
> The world revolved from night to day,
> A voice, a chime, a chant sublime
> Of peace on earth, goodwill to men.
> — *Henry W. Longfellow*[8]

A CHRISTMAS STORY OF JESUS [9]

Come and take a trip with me! We are going across seas and over many miles of land far, far away to a little country named Judea. It would take us a long time to get there if it were not for jet planes.

We are not only going far away from our home here in America, but we are going back into the past, a long, long time ago. We are going back almost 2,000 years. To do this we must give up many things. We must give up our automobiles, airplanes, and rockets. We must give up our electricity, our television sets, our refrigerators, and our air conditioners.

In America in that far-off time there are no cities and no towns. The country is a wilderness. The country is like the deepest woods you have ever been in. There are no white men here, only tribes of Indians. *We* are not here. We are in Palestine 2,000 years ago in the time of Jesus.

No one really knows what happened when Jesus was born. No one who was really there at the time told about it. There were no writers to write about it. But men who lived after Jesus died tried to imagine what might have happened. Now that we are there, we can imagine it too.

We can see Mary and Joseph wearily traveling the miles between

[8] *Complete Poetical Works*, Horace E. Scudder, ed. (Boston: Houghton Mifflin Company, 1948).

[9] Used by permission of the Hartford School of Religious Education.

Nazareth and Bethlehem, only to find on their arrival that the city is very crowded and it is hard to find a place to spend the night. After they find a place to stay, the baby Jesus is born. We can imagine the baby nestling in his mother's arms while she and Joseph look down at him with loving, joy-filled faces. When a healthy baby is born, it is always a time of great happiness. We can see the people from nearby trooping in to see the baby who has just been born on this clear, starry night in Bethlehem. This is the birth of a baby who will grow up to be the greatest man the world has ever known.

Jesus is a Jewish boy, and he is brought up in a Jewish home. Here, in his home in Nazareth, Jesus lives with his mother Mary and his father Joseph, with his sisters and his four brothers. Here we find him playing on the flat-topped roof of his home, climbing fig trees, playing games, hiking over the trails and hills around Nazareth and looking over the countryside.

Jesus celebrates the Sabbath with his family and goes to services at the Jewish synagogue with his father. He says Jewish prayers; he studies with his teachers about Jewish customs and laws, and about God. He studies the part of the Bible which we know as the Old Testament. This is his Bible. The New Testament was not yet written; that was done long after he had lived in Palestine.

Joseph is a carpenter; and, like all Jewish boys, Jesus learns his father's trade so that one day he too may become a carpenter. He spends much of his time in his father's carpenter shop helping him make many things.

As Jesus grows up he learns a great deal about God. He feels God's greatness and God's great love for all people. He wonders about God's plan for people and the way God wants people to live.

Jesus becomes so excited about what he learns of God and believes in God's love and greatness so deeply that he wants to share with all people the wonderful things he has discovered about God.

Jesus is now 30 years old. He is a man. He leaves his home in Nazareth; he leaves his family and his work as a carpenter, and travels around the country of Palestine, teaching people about God and the way God wants people to live. He chooses twelve men to help him teach. These men become his closest friends and travel with him everywhere he goes.

Many people listen to Jesus! They believe in him and come to love him. These people become Jesus' pupils and followers and try to live the way Jesus teaches them to live.

Some people do not understand him and do not believe in him. They fear and dislike him. One night a few of these people seize him when he is alone with his friends, and in the end he is put to death.

But Jesus is so close to God and is so loved by his followers that even death cannot put an end to his life and teaching. Those men and women who have become his followers keep up the work which Jesus has begun. The people who have known him join together and tell others of his life and his teaching about God and form churches.

We are still doing these things today in our own time and in our country — and in other countries all over the world.

Because Jesus lived 2,000 years ago in a little country far away, the whole world has been made different. Through Jesus, people have come to understand what God is like and how he wishes people to live.

— Shirley Miller

THEME X
HOW TO WORK WITH THE ETERNAL LAWS OF GOD

1. Readings after concreteness:

You will know the truth, and the truth shall make you free.
— John 8:32

Seek first his kingdom and his righteousness.
— Matthew 6:33a

The ordinances of the Lord are true and righteous altogether, More to be desired are they than gold, even much fine gold.
— Psalm 19:9b, 10

(Use also Psalm 8:1, 3-9.)

2. Closing Prayer

From thee all skill and science flow,
All pity, care and love
All calm and courage, faith and hope;
O pour them from above.

And part them, Lord, to each and all,
As each and all shall need,
To rise like incense, each to thee,
In noble thought and deed. . . .

And hasten, Lord, that perfect day
When pain and death shall cease,
And thy just rule shall fill the earth,
With health and light and peace.[10]

— *Charles Kingsley*

Incline my heart to thy testimonies,
and not to gain!
Turn my eyes from looking at vanities
And give me life in thy ways.

— *Psalm 119:36, 37*

3. Closing Hymn: "The Spacious Firmament" or "These Things Shall Be"

CONTINUATION OF THEME X

Write to the Metropolitan Life Insurance Company offices, New York City, for a series of stories, "Health Heroes."

THEME XI. THE PRICE OF FREEDOM

Introductory Music . . . fade out.

ANNOUNCER: It is a quiet day in Denmark. A deceptive quiet. For beneath the surface, there is a stirring of the people under the iron hand of the Occupation. In a small Jutland village, the gate of the Parsonage opens. A man comes running up the path *(Sound of running footsteps, which stops abruptly. Urgent pounding on the door.)*

HENRIK: *(calling out)* Pastor Munk . . . Pastor Munk . . . *(Squeaking of a door opening rapidly. Door closes.)*

HENRIK: Pastor Munk . . . it is very serious . . . the police are coming down the road . . . they are coming here . . . to this house.

MUNK: I knew that some day they would come.

HENRIK: But why? We have not antagonized the Germans. Denmark has hardly resisted them . . .

MUNK: That is our sin, Henrik, the sin of Denmark. Too many of our people have mistaken the voice of Hitler for the voice of God.

HENRIK: Pastor!

(Fade in sound of marching; steady increase, then halt.)

---

10 "Gifts of Healing" by Charles Kingsley, *The Pilgrim Hymnal* (Boston: Pilgrim Press, 1958). Used by permission.

HENRIK: *(Undertone)* They're here. What will you do, Pastor?

MUNK: As a follower of Christ, I "must obey God rather than man."

(Loud pounding on door. Door squeaks, opens slowly.)

MUNK: You wish to see me? I am the Pastor.

POLICE: Yes, I come from the Ministry. It is learned that you intend to mention in your sermon tomorrow something about the activities of the Norwegian church. That is strictly forbidden, Pastor Munk.

MUNK: Yes, Lieutenant, my sympathy for the suffering of my brothers in Norway . . .

POLICE: To speak of it in public is strictly forbidden. I warn you . . . to disobey will mean defiance of the Third Reich.

MUNK: It is indeed considerate of you, Lieutenant.

POLICE: Do you intend to obey that order?

MUNK: I give you my word. . . . In my sermon tomorrow I will shun all but the truth.

(Organ playing religious music . . . fade out.)

MUNK: *(from pulpit)* Now, while we are all assembled together in our church, let me reveal to you that I have been told not to mention the struggle of those our Norwegian brethren. Not to speak of them! Oh, were I to sit down as a passive spectator because of fear of men, I should feel myself a traitor to my Christian faith. Rather let us pray! Give us Christianity, give us courage and faith to rise out of despondence and fickleness to will only that which is right, no matter what the cost. Lead us, thou cross in our flag, lead us into the struggle where shackled Norway fights against principles which are directly opposed to all our principles. I will close with the words of Martin Luther: "Here I stand, I cannot do otherwise. For it is not safe for a man to act against his conscience."

(Heavy footsteps approach and stop)

POLICE: *(shouting)* Everyone remain seated where they are. This man has rebelled. He was given warning and instruction. He has defied the Third Reich.

(Sound of heavy boots treading up the church aisle.
Sound ceases abruptly.)

POLICE: Pastor Munk . . .

MUNK: Do you dare to interfere with the preaching of the truth in the House of God?

POLICE: Pastor Munk, I arrest you . . .

VOICE OF CROWD: Arrest? the Pastor?

(Voices rise again in general murmur.)

POLICE: *(Above the crowd)* It is by order of the Third Reich.

VOICES OF CROWD: They shall not do it . . . We won't let them . . . No . . . No.

MUNK: Peace, my brethren, fear only defiance of God

(Voices become silent again.)

MUNK: But prepare yourselves to save the many. Remember . . . things will not be better in Denmark until the Danish people have learned their lesson from the courage of Christ.

POLICE: Come on . . . enough of words.

MUNK: *(Crying out)* Courage, my people . . . "A mighty fortress is our God . . ."

(Organ strikes up "A Mighty Fortress." Voices take it up in song. Fade down sharply to background.)

ANNOUNCER: A few weeks passed during which time Pastor Munk was under house arrest. And then . . .

(Knock at door, door opens.)

POLICE: Come with us, Pastor Munk.

MUNK: What are you going to do to me?

POLICE: I have orders. . . . Get in. Don't try to trick us.

(Car door slams. Car starts with a roar. Up sound of car at high speed, then fade to steady background.)

MUNK: Where are you taking me?

POLICE: *(Exaggerated politeness)* Out of the village, Pastor. A little ride.

MUNK: Since you arrested me by order of the state authorities, you should take me to them.

POLICE: I can rescind the order, Pastor. That is why I wish to have a little chat with you.

MUNK: To do this way is necessary. I demand that you take me back. . . .

POLICE: A ride in an automobile, Pastor, is sometimes more conducive to straight talking.

MUNK: Speak the truth, Lieutenant. It is not for conversation that you have me kidnapped.

POLICE: *(Sharply)* I do not like that word, Pastor.

MUNK: Can you deny it?

POLICE: *(Menacing)* So . . . It is for you to speak the truth. Are you prepared to give me your word that from now on you will cooperate?

MUNK: I will cooperate with none but God.

POLICE: Answer me. I give you your last chance. Do you intend continued resistance to the Third Reich?

MUNK: I will forever be faithful to the truth as revealed in the Word of God. And those who seek to coerce me by violence, and by . . .

POLICE: *(Breaking in)* Silence. Stop the car.

(Car comes to a grinding stop)

POLICE: Get out, Pastor Munk.

(Sound of car door being opened)

MUNK: I have one request, Lieutenant.

POLICE: *(Sneering)* You have decided to change your mind?

MUNK: Let me kneel here on the soil of my country and pray. *(Praying)* O God, take into thy great heart this land and its people. Give my people courage to resist the evil, not to compromise with unrighteousness. Grant us courage to become wholly loyal to that which we believe. Though the prisons be filled to the point of bursting, though —

(Sharp report of revolver breaking off his words.
Car door slams. Car roars away. Fade out.)

ANNOUNCER: And so Denmark lost a great leader to the cause of freedom. The Pastor lay dead, but the spirit of Kaj Munk fights on in his people.[11]

THEME XII. FINDING FREEDOM

Processional: "For the Beauty of the Earth"

Call to Worship:

O Lord, how manifold are thy works!
In wisdom hast thou made them all;
The earth is full of thy creatures . . . .
I will sing to the Lord as long as I live. . . .

— *Psalm 104:24, 33*

O give thanks unto the Lord, for he is good;
for his steadfast love endures forever!

— *Psalm 107:1*

Thank the Lord for his steadfast love,
for his wonderful works to the sons of men.

— *Psalm 107:21*

[11] Permission to use this broadcast was graciously given by Rev. Henry Smith Leiper, World Council of Churches, New York.

Response: "Sanctus."

Offering:

> Now, we will give our offering. We are glad to bring our gifts of money today because we have freedom to come to the church and worship God as we think is right.

Offering Hymn: "We Give Thee but Thine Own."

Story: Statue of Liberty (below)

Scripture Reading:
Let us love one another; for love is of God . . . .
> — *1 John 4:7*

He who loves God should love his brother also.
> — *1 John 4:21b*

Love is patient and kind; love is not jealous or boastful; it is not arrogant, or rude. Love does not insist on its own way; it is not irritable or resentful; it does not rejoice at wrong, but rejoices in the right.
> — *1 Corinthians 13:4-6*

He who abides in love abides in God . . . .
> — *1 John 4:16b*

Prayer:

> Our God, we thank thee that France and the United States are friends. May all the nations of the world be friends and kind and loving to each other.
> We thank three that our country welcomes people from the other parts of the world. May she continue to receive these people. May each one of us be like Jesus, who loves everybody. Amen.

Response: Threefold Amen.

Recessional: "America the Beautiful"

STATUE OF LIBERTY

Years ago, some people of France wanted to do something for the United States. They said, "America is celebrating the 100th year of her independence. She loves freedom and we love freedom.

We helped her gain her independence. We are friends. What shall we do to show our friendship toward her?" So the people thought and thought, trying to find out what they could do. Several made suggestions but they were not too good. Finally one said, "I have an idea. Let us give her a statue which represents that America stands for freedom and that freedom brings light to all people." "Why, that is a marvelous idea," everybody chorused.

"But," they said, scratching their heads, "where will we get the money to do that? The statue has to be a very big one in order that people can see it very easily." "I know," someone answered. "We will tell all the people of France about it; they will be happy to give money."

So they told the people about the project and the people gave willingly. A French sculptor was asked to make plans for this very big statue.

When the people of America heard about the plan of France, they said, "We want to do something; we want to have a share in your wonderful plan. While you build that statue, we will build the pedestal where your statue will stand." The people in America also made their contributions very willingly.

The work was started in France. One year passed, and the statue was not even half finished. The second year passed, and still it was not finished. Then people worked harder and harder in order that it would be finished. The third year passed, and the fourth; still it was not finished. Then, at the end of five long years, the great statue was finally finished and ready to be taken across the ocean to America. The people of France loaded it in a boat and the boat carried it to New York Harbor, where the pedestal had already been prepared on an island. With big iron supports, the big statue from France was put in place.

The big day came when the statue was to be unveiled and dedicated. People from many parts of America came for that important day. People from France crossed the Atlantic to be there when the statue would be presented to the American people. Finally, the veil was taken away, and lo, the Statue of Liberty stood in its beauty and majesty, a woman holding a big torch, "Liberty Enlightening the World."

But wait, what are those words at the base of the Statue?

There was a Jewish woman, Emma Lazarus by name. She was an American poet. Many Jews were fleeing from Russia because they were treated cruelly. Emma saw these homeless and hungry Jews finding shelter in America. She wrote poems about these poor people, and also gave herself to the task of caring for them.

Emma did not have only the Jews in mind, but all the homeless and hungry people of Europe, when she wrote those words which we now find at the base of the Statue of Liberty. She saw America opening her arms to all people who want freedom and opportunity to live better lives. Hear America speaking:

> "Give me your tired, your poor
> Your huddled masses yearning to breathe free,
> The wretched refuse of your teeming shore,
> Send these, the homeless, tempest-tost to me;
> I lift my lamp beside the golden door."

ROGER WILLIAMS

"Mother, why do people go to different churches? The Roman Catholics go to their church, the Jews go to their synagogue, and we go to our Protestant church. Can we not force the Roman Catholics and the Jews to go to our church?" asked Johnny one night.

With loving eyes, mother looked at Johnny and said, "Johnny, many years ago there were people who left their homes in England and other countries of Europe because they were not allowed to worship God as they thought was right. They came to the United States when this country was still wilderness, sickness was everywhere, there were many wild beasts, and there was not much food; but they stayed because they could worship God freely. But some of these people did not allow others to worship God in their own way. They oppressed the Roman Catholics, the Jews, and the other Protestants who did not follow everything they did.

"Then there was one man who thought that this was not right. They had left their homes in England and Europe in order that they could worship God freely; now they should allow others to worship God in their own way. So this man, a minister, went to Rhode Island, and there he received all kinds of people into his colony and into his church. This man was Roger Williams."

"How did he do that, mother?" asked Johnny.

"Well, let me tell you a story about Roger Williams," replied mother.

"One very stormy night, Reuben was staggering through the blinding snow. He hugged his little son Benjamin close to his heart and prayed that he might find a house. His body was aching with cold; and he was very hungry, for he had not eaten since morning.

"Suddenly Benjamin awoke and said, 'Father I am very cold and hungry.' His father said, 'Be patient, little one; soon we will find a lodging for the night. Surely no one would turn even a Jew away in a storm like this.'

"The father struggled through the storm, then, exhausted, he fell. The weight of little Benjamin in his arms aroused him, so he struggled to get up, and walked on. Then he came to a little shack. A tallow candle shone through the window. He was so exhausted that he fell against the door and knew nothing more.

"He awoke and looked around. He found that he was resting upon a couch of skins, with a soft, warm blanket over him. It was a poor place; the walls were bare and there were only a few chairs and a rough table for furniture. Near the table sat two men. One wore rich clothing with a broad, white collar; this man was holding little Benjamin on his knee feeding him. The other was in gray clothing.

"Reuben wondered. 'What kind of men are these who treat a Jewish wanderer so kindly?' 'Shalom,' said the man in gray, smiling.

"'Shalom, aleichem,' answered Reuben. 'But you are not a Jew.'

"'No, but I am a minister and I have studied the Hebrew language. I love its greeting of "Peace." Would that my people were lovers of peace, even as yours have been so long.'

"Little Benjamin ran to his father. 'Father, the good man gave me some warm milk and bread, and this coat to wear.'

"The man in gray placed food and drink on the table for Reuben, who was still wondering if he were dreaming. When had Christians given him food and shelter and received him with gentle words?

"The man in rich clothing said, 'I fled from Spain because I was going to be killed. I am a devout Catholic and did not deserve such hatred. I came here, but those who are not Roman Catholics despise me. They drove me away, but here in Rhode Island, Roger Williams has given me the hand of brotherhood.'

"The man in gray arose and held out his hand to the Jewish wanderer. 'And now, I give my hand in friendship to you. My colony of Rhode Island has need of men strong enough to die — yes, to live for the faith they will be allowed to follow here. This day you have found a refuge with me and my people.'

"Little by little the winds outside ceased and there was silence. The Spaniard walked to the window and said, 'Dawn is breaking.' Bowing reverently, he began to tell his beads as he recited his morning prayer. Roger Williams took his large Bible, and knelt beside his chair to pray. Reuben led little Benjamin to the window. He drew his faded prayer shawl over his shoulders and, facing the east, praised the God of Israel who had led him through many dangers to this place of refuge." [12]

THOMAS HOOKER

Today is the Founders' Day of this church. This church [Center Church, Hartford, Connecticut] was established because there were men, women, and children who were brave and unafraid; because there were men and women and children who believed in God.

More than 300 years ago, many people left their homes in England because they were not allowed to worship God according to what they believed was right. "Let us go to America," they said. "There, in that faraway land, we can worship God freely, and nobody will hurt us."

So they took a boat. Their boat was not as big as our boats today. It was not as fast as ours, so that it took many days before they reached Boston. Sometimes the waves were big and the children had to stay in bed because they did not feel well.

Finally they reached Boston. They started working on their farms but they were not able to harvest much. The first winter was very hard; it was very cold and they did not have much to eat.

They built a meeting house in what is now called Cambridge. They wrote to Thomas Hooker, "Please, come to us now and be our minister."

Thomas Hooker was in Holland because he was driven out of England. "I am going to America and be the minister of those people," he said. So with Samuel Stone he left for America. On the boat, they sang hymns, they prayed, and they talked about God to their companions.

After six weeks, they reached the shores of the United States. The people went to the shore to meet Thomas Hooker. They were very happy because their minister had arrived. "Welcome to the land of the free!" they cried. They were so happy that a month later they had a big celebration, giving thanks to God for his kindness.

One year later, Thomas Hooker and the members of his church decided to transfer to Connecticut. Many people advised them not to leave. "Connecticut is still wilderness; there is no road going

---

[12] Adaptation from "A Place of Refuge," in *The New Land* by Elma Ehrlich Levinger, (New York: Block Publishing Company, 1920).

there, there are many savage Indians," they warned. But the travelers decided to go.

They packed their few utensils, their clothes, and a supply of food. The day came. The children were excited. "We are going to Connecticut!" they exclaimed. The men put their packs on their backs, the mothers carried the babies, and the older boys drove the 160 head of cattle. There were about a hundred men, women, and children in all. Mrs. Hooker was carried upon a litter. Maybe she was not well.

They walked and walked through thick forests, over mountains, across valleys, and through swamps, thickets, and rivers. The children became very tired and they started to cry: "I'm tired." "I'm hungry." "I can't walk any more." So the people stopped and rested. The boys gathered some dry wood and leaves and built the fire. The women and the girls cooked the food. Everybody ate, and the children stopped crying.

At night they slept in the open. There were no houses on the way where they could stay. The men and boys gathered plenty of leaves of the trees and put them on the ground; then the mothers spread blankets on top of these. For shelter, another blanket with corners tied to four sticks was over them. The men guarded the sleeping children and women with their guns against wild beasts and savage Indians.

After two weeks and one hundred miles of foot travel, they reached the place which they called Hartford. They started cutting the trees of the forest for their farms. They built their log cabins. Their first church building was a plain square structure, located near the present site of the Old State House.

The present church building is the fourth one. It has been changed four times already.

Very soon, we will pay a visit to the Burying Ground. It is the place where Thomas Hooker and many others who helped in founding this church were buried. We are glad that through them we can come to this church and worship God as we think is right.

PRAYER

Our God, we thank thee for this day when we celebrate the founding of this church. We thank thee for the men, women, and children who many years ago hiked through wilderness and mountains, suffering hunger in order that they could come to Hartford and found this church. We thank thee for Thomas Hooker, who led them and inspired them and guided them to this place. May

each one of us help to make this church a church for everybody, where each one can worship thee freely. May we help other people to come to thee through this church. In Jesus' name, Amen.

Some Worship Services for Children (8-12 Years)

THEME: ALL PEOPLE ARE GOD'S CHILDREN

Processional: "Joyful, Joyful, We Adore Thee"

(Sung by an interracial children's chorus)

Call to Worship: (May be given as a chorus by a class seated in the choir wearing gowns, or the leader)

The earth is the Lord's and the fulness thereof.
the world, and those who dwell therein.

— Psalm 24:1

The earth is full of the loving kindness of the Lord,
For his loving kindness endureth forever.
See what love the father has given us,
that we should be called children of God; and so we are.

— 1 John 3:1

Introit Response: Sanctus from "The Holy City," by Alfred R. Gaul:
Holy, Holy, Holy Lord of Hosts;
Holy, Holy, Holy is the Lord of Hosts. Amen.

Hymn: "God's Children Live in Many Lands."

Story: "People's Color Is Only Skin Deep," from *All About Us* by Eva Knox Evans, (New York: Capitol Publishing Co., 1947), pp. 11-22, 27-31, 89-92. (A series of services can be developed from this book.)

Choral Reading: (By a class reading as a chorus or by the leader or as solos by a group standing together.)
And he made from one every nation of men to live on all the face of the earth.

— Acts 17:26

Paul said, "Decide never to put a stumblingblock or hindrance in the way of a brother."

— Romans 14:13

John said, "Let us love one another; for love is of God . . . he who loves God should love his brother also."

— 1 John 4:7a, 21b

Paul said, "Love is patient and kind; love is not jealous or boastful; it is not arrogant or rude. Love does not insist on its own way; it is not irritable or resentful; it does not rejoice at wrong, but rejoices in the right.

— 1 Corinthians 13:4-6

Jesus said, "This is my commandment, that you love one another as I have loved you . . . . You are my friends if you do what I command you . . . . Love one another . . . ."

— John 15:12, 14, 17b

By this all men will know that you are my disciples, if you have love for one another.

— John 13:35

Prayer:

O God, we are glad that we are your children and that you love us so very much.

O God, we are sorry for the many times we forget to show your love to other people.

O God, we are sorry that so many people are unhappy and injured because some of us are unkind and thoughtless.

O God, we are glad to remember that your way of love includes all kinds of people.

O God, we wish to begin to show more of your love to more of your children. We thank you for trusting us so much to make the world like a big family of brothers.

Hymn: "O Brother Man, Fold to Thy Heart Thy Brother." (Tune: *Ancient of Days*) One stanza with Amen.

Benediction or Recessional

THEME: OUR DEBT TO THE MIGRANTS

Call to Worship

Hymn: "Joyful, Joyful, We Adore Thee"

Story: "I Am Haunted by the Migrants

Scripture for Choral Reading:
When a stranger sojourns with you in your land, you shall not
do him wrong. The stranger who sojourns with you shall be to
you as the native among you, and you shall love him as yourself.

— Leviticus 19:33-34a

Choral Reading:
God created America, a land of hope and dreams,
He filled it with broad, rolling prairies,
    and sprinkled it with swift and flowing streams,
Tall mountains, vast forests, he placed here,
    and then from the ends of the earth —
He called people of all races,
Each bearing a gift of worth.

— Anonymous

Prayer

Hymn: "O Brother Man, Fold to Thy Heart Thy Brother."

Benediction:

Our Father, may our hands work for thee, and may the peace
that passeth all understanding be known in the hearts of all
people. Amen.

Postlude

I AM HAUNTED BY THE MIGRANTS

My kitchen is full these days of uninvited guests. In vain I try
to ignore them, to pretend they are not there. Quietly, persistently
they follow me about, startling me in unexpected places, reappear-
ing suddenly at every turn I make, emerging out of nothingness.
(Pause)
I take a head of lettuce from the ice box, but as I hold it in my
hands, about to break it into cups for salad, it suddenly becomes
the tousled head of a little child bending patiently over long rows
of lettuce stretching across a sun-baked field. I see small hands
blistered from the handle of the cutting knife and a bent back
that never will be straight.
(Pause)
I'm squeezing oranges for breakfast juice, and, as I reach for
another, a woman hands it to me from a ladder propped against
a tree of golden balls. "I hope it makes your children strong and

well," she says. "My baby lying yonder in that spot of shade grows thinner every day."

I'm picking over cranberries for sauce. I feel a tugging at my skirt, and turn with hands full of the shiny red marbles to see the freckled face and big eyes of a boy beseeching me, "Put them in Ma's box, please! I'm helping her to fill it. When it's full, they'll give us fifteen cents. Pa says if we'll pick fast enough, we can buy gas to get us back to Oysters."

(Pause)

A cup of sugar poured into a bowl for mixing cakes becomes in spite of me the white hair of a man, not old, but aged with struggles far beyond the strength of youth to bear. "We were topping beets when my wife died. Her heart give out. It never was too strong. She couldn't stand the long hours in the heat. Now I've got to raise the kids alone, raise 'em for what, I wonder — to go on topping beets and dyin' like their Ma did?"

(Pause)

Tomatoes are no better. They turn perversely into rows and rows of faces flushed with flaming red, with fever and with rash. " 'Twas in the tomato farms where they all had measles," a woman is explaining, her eyes full of weariness and pain. "The whole camp had it. That's why the nurse just couldn't get to Pete before he died. If only she had come in time! But I don't know — if he'd got well, he might have gone with Sue, with scarlet fever, later in Asparagus."

(Pause)

Prunes poured into a pan to soak have a mysterious way of developing arms and legs, and quickly scramble out onto the shelf to stare at me with the dark and questioning faces of Mexican children. "Where did you come from?" I ask, startled. "Are you Americans?" "We were born in Prunes," they say. "Is that America?" (Pause) "No," I shout so fiercely that they are frightened out of themselves and turn to prunes again. "No! America is a place where children are born to freedom and to equality of opportunity, to a chance for school and church, to a chance to have enough to eat and decent clothes to wear, to a chance for work that leaves a little time to play, to a chance for health and happiness! This is not America. Someone must do something about this un-American way of life!"

(Pause)

My own healthy, happy children come trooping in for dinner. We sit down to a plentiful meal, good to taste, and rich in vitamins. Crowding into our comfortable family circle, and looking wistfully over our shoulders, come hundreds of people — men and women, boys and girls, hungry, weary, homeless, denied a share in the bountiful plenty that they have helped to create. Wanderers over the face of the earth are these migrant workers of the crops. No home but a broken-down old car or a shack hastily put together with materials from a junk pile. The children attend school only here and there, now and then. No church. No doctors. No chance at cleanliness or beauty in their lives. Always hungry. Always afraid. (Pause)

What can I do about it? I shrug my shoulders and tell myself "nothing," but it doesn't work. These ghosts of my disinherited brothers of the crops haunt me through all my days. I try upon myself the arguments I have heard complacently put forth. "It's their own fault. If they tried hard enough to get a better job, of course they could." "They don't mind living like that. They're used to it."

But the arguments are hollow and unreal and the human need remains. No, I must discover something to do about it if I am to live at peace with my own soul and with the uninvited guests that crowd my kitchen.

— *Estella Lane* [13]

THEME: HOW IT FEELS TO BE COLORED

Worship Center:

A table set with two candles and a picture of a great American Negro, preferably James Weldon Johnson. Behind this picture, a map of the United States.

Prelude: "Where Cross the Crowded Ways"
(played very softly)

Call to Worship:

Offering: 1. Motivation
2. Prayer

Story: "How It Feels To Be Colored" [14]

[13] From *Children's Religion*, February, 1940. Copyright, The Pilgrim Press. Used by permission.

[14] From *The Autobiography of an Ex-Colored Man*. New York: Alfred A. Knopf Inc., 1927. Used by permission.

Hymn: Negro Anthem, "Lift Every Voice and Sing."
Words by James Weldon Johnson.
(Words and music may be secured from Cooperative Recreation Service, Delaware, Ohio)

Response in Unison: Romans 12:1, 2, 9 or Leviticus 19:17, 18.

Poem:
The crest and crowning of all good,
Life's final star is brotherhood;
For it will bring again to Earth
Her long-lost Poesy and Mirth,
Will send new light on every face,
A kingly power upon the race,
And till it comes, we men are slaves,
And travel downward to the dust of graves.
Come, clear the way then, clear the way:
Blind creeds and kings have had their day.
Break the dead branches from the path;
Our hope is in the aftermath —
Our hope is in heroic men,
Star-led to build the world again.
To this Event the ages ran:
Make way for Brotherhood — make way for Man.
— *Edwin Markham* [15]

HOW IT FEELS TO BE COLORED

One day at the end of my second term at school, the principal came into our room and, after talking to the teacher, for some reason said: "I wish all of the white scholars to stand for a moment." I rose with the others. The teacher looked at me and, calling my name, said, "You sit down for the present and rise with the others." I did not quite understand her, and questioned? "Ma'am?" She repeated with a softer tone in her voice: "You sit down now and rise with the others." I sat down dazed; I saw and heard nothing. When the others were asked to rise, I did not know it. When school was dismissed, I went out in a kind of stupor. A few of the white boys jeered me, saying, "Oh, you're a nigger too." I heard some black children say, "We knew he was colored." Shiny said to them: "Come along, don't tease him," and thereby won my undying gratitude.

[15] "Brotherhood." Used by permission of Virgil Markham.

I hurried on as fast as I could . . . and ran into the house. As I passed through the hallway, I saw that my mother was busy with one of her customers. I rushed up into my own little room, shut the door, and went quickly to where my looking-glass hung on the wall. For an instant I was afraid to look, but I did; I looked long and earnestly. I had often heard people say to my mother, "What a pretty boy you have!" . . . I noticed . . . the beauty of my mouth, the size and liquid darkness of my eyes, and how the long, black lashes that fringed and shaded them produced an effect that was strangely fascinating even to me. I noticed the softness and glossiness of my dark hair that fell in waves over my temples . . . I ran downstairs and rushed to where my mother was sitting . . . I buried my head in her lap and blurted out: "Mother, mother, tell me, am I a nigger?" I could not see her face, but I knew the piece of work dropped to the floor and I felt her hands on my head . . . . There were tears in her eyes and I could see that she was suffering for me.

And then it was that I looked at her critically for the first time. I had thought of her in a childish way only as the most beautiful woman in the world; now I looked at her searching for defects. I could see that her skin was brown, that her hair was not so soft as mine, and that she did differ in some way from the other ladies who came to the house; yet even so I could see that she was very beautiful, more beautiful than any of them.

And so I have often lived through that hour, that day, that week. . . . From that time I looked out through other eyes, my thoughts were colored, my words dictated, my actions limited by one dominating, all-pervading idea . . . until I finally realized in it a great tangible fact.

And this is the dwarfing, warping, distorting influence which operates upon each and every colored man in the United States. He is forced to take his outlook on all things, not from the viewpoint of a citizen, or a man, or even a human being, but from the viewpoint of a colored man.

— *James Weldon Johnson*

A SIXTH GRADE LEARNS ABOUT GOD

As a result of a study of worship in the Old Testament and some experiences in visiting a synagogue and a Roman Catholic service, a sixth grade created a climax program. Here is their summary of some of their conclusions.

CHORUS: For countless years men have known God,
But their ideas of God have changed.

LEADER: Thousands of years ago, the Hebrew people wandered
from place to place.
They thought of God as a god of war and revenge.
When the Hebrews settled in Palestine, their idea of God
changed.
They crowned King Saul, then David was king.
They thought of Jehovah as a god of agriculture.

CHORUS: Men's ideas of God have changed,
But God is still the same.

LEADER: Men's ideas of God have changed greatly through the
centuries.
Amos told of a God of righteousness;
Hosea told men of a God of love.
Isaiah preached about a God who loved all people.
The story of Ruth tells of how men learned to be friendly
to foreigners.
Then came Jesus.
He taught men of a loving Father-God.

CHORUS: Men's ideas of God have changed,
But God is still the same.

LEADER: Men have worshiped God in many places and ways.
The Hebrews who lived in the desert worshiped God in
high places.
They worshiped him with ceremonies and sacrifices.
Some people built temples in which to worship God.
The Jewish people worshiped God in Jerusalem for many
years
The first synagogue was built during the time of the Exile.

CHORUS: Men's ways of worship have changed,
But God is still the same.

LEADER: Today men worship God in many ways.
We visited a synagogue in which our Jewish friends wor-
ship.
There we saw the Rabbi.
We saw the scrolls and the Torah, which is the code of
laws.
The seats looked like theater seats.
Their prayer book is partly in Hebrew.
One of their symbols is the Star of David.
The Jewish Sabbath begins on Friday evening.

Special prayers are said in the home on the Sabbath,
And special food is eaten.
The Jewish people have special Holy Days.
Rosh Hashanah is the beginning of the Jewish New Year.
This festival lasts ten days and ends on a day called Yom Kippur.
The Passover comes at Easter time.
The people eat kosher food during these Holy Days.

CHORUS: Men have worshiped God in many ways,
But God is still the same.

LEADER: In the Roman Catholic Church their service is called the mass.
It is said 'n Latin.
They have crucifixes and statues in their churches.
The people often use rosaries when they pray.
They confess their sins to the priest,
And the priest assigns a penance which they must do
To pay for their sins.
Their churches have 14 pictures with crosses above them.
They are called the stations of the cross.
They celebrate Christmas and Easter,
But they also have many other Holy Days.
They say grace at the table in their homes as we do.

CHORUS: Men have worshiped God in many ways,
But God remains the same.

LEADER: In our church the services are in English.
We have an empty cross in our church.
To symbolize the living Christ.
We say our prayers directly to God and ask him to forgive us.
It is our responsibility to make up for our sins by apologizing for them
And by promising never to do them again.
In our homes grace is said at the table.

CHORUS: Men have worshiped God in many ways,
But God is still the same.

LEADER: Our Father,
We are thankful that men have known thee for thousands of years,
And that their ideas of thee have grown.
We are thankful for the different ways men worship;
For our Jewish friends who worship in the synagogue,

And have their Sabbath on Saturday.
For our Roman Catholic neighbors who have special holy
days and Communion every Sunday.
For our own church where we worship and study every
Sunday.

CHORUS: People worship God in many ways,
But he is still the same.
Amen.

A Service of Personal Dedication

Call to Worship

Hymn: "Spirit of God Descend upon My Heart"

A Christian Vow (in unison)

I will strive each day to live a simple, sincere, and serene life;
repelling promptly every thought of discontent, anxiety and
discouragement, impurity and self-seeking; I will seek inspiration from the beauty of God's earth and the companionship of
worthy friends. I will be creative, counting it a privilege to
enrich and ennoble each day with all the talent God has given
me. I will have no traffic in cheap thoughts or acts, but from
the mind God has given me shall come forth that which brings
uplift to others and honor to his name. I will be cheerful,
courteous, and charitable to others; yet, in that charity, no
weakening pity shall go forth to one in need, but only that
comfort which is strength and courage. If wrong shall come to
another through me, I shall seek pardon and forgiveness, being
sure to forgive others before they ask. I will seek God's will to
make it mine. I will remember in prayer the children of all
nations. I will emulate the Christ, that he may have many who
will witness to the joy of Christian living.

Scripture Reading

Prayer

O God, our Father, we thank thee for the sanctity of all our days
lived in the security of thy care. Thou dost lead us in ways we
know not, but to follow in high sacrificial courage is to know
why. In this hour of the world's dire need, make us helpers,
one of another, in every sacred call of duty. We believe that

each life is a sanctuary of truth and love, and that each heart may be an inner room of holiness. We believe that we have been called to a high task, and that ours is a solemn responsibility, and that the measure of the hour's need is the measure of the dedication to which thou hast called us. Amen.

Hymn: "God Send Us Men"

Benediction

Index